• SUPERTAROT •

By the same author:
BODY READING
FORTUNE-TELLING BY TAROT CARDS
FORTUNE-TELLING BY TEA LEAVES
LIVING PALMISTRY (with Malcolm Wright)
MOON SIGNS
RISING SIGNS
SUN SIGNS
TAROT IN ACTION!
UNDERSTANDING ASTROLOGY

SUPER TAROT

New techniques for improving your Tarot reading

SASHA FENTON

Aquarian/Thorsons

An Imprint of HarperCollins*Publishers*

The Aquarian Press
An Imprint of HarperCollins*Publishers*
77–85 Fulham Palace Road,
Hammersmith, London W6 8JB

Published by The Aquarian Press 1991
3 5 7 9 10 8 6 4

A catalogue record for this book
is available from the British Library

ISBN 1 85538 017 X

Typeset by Harper Phototypsetters Limited,
Northampton, England
Printed in Great Britain by
Woolnough Bookbinding Limited,
Irthlingborough, Northamptonshire

Dedication

To Elizabeth Richardson without whom none of my books would have been written. Good luck with your books, Elizabeth!

Acknowledgements

To Helen, Stuart and Tony Fenton for all their support, help and for being guinea-pigs for my experiments. To all my other guinea-pigs, including Simon Pamplin, Anne Christie, Denise Russell, Judith Stewart and Simon Franklin. To Frank Anderson for proof reading and to Linda Tully for sorting out the muddles and doing so much of the typing. Also to Barry Belasco for encouraging me to put the ideas into practice.

Contents

Introduction

What is This Book All About?

This book has been designed and written in response to many requests which I have had over the years from people who manage to learn the meanings of the Tarot cards off by heart but then find that they cannot put them together to make a worthwhile interpretation. The ideas, advice, exercises and games in this book are designed to help you overcome this problem once and for all. Some of the teaching methods have come out of the successful series of Tarot workshops run in the south of England by Eve Bingham and myself, while others have come straight from my own convoluted mind.

The best way to use this book is to start on page one and work your way through it in the same way that you would study a school textbook. You will get more out of the book by working through it in this way than by dipping into pages at random, because it has been designed to give you specific information and advice when you need it and to lead you through graded stages of attainment. You will need the co-operation of a couple of friends for some of the experiments because you cannot learn Tarot without checking your progress on other people. I doubt whether you will have any difficulty in finding willing guinea-pigs because practically everybody loves having their cards read, even by someone who is still learning the craft. There are a number of games which are all carefully designed to stretch your imagination and to encourage you to become more relaxed and confident when using the cards. One of the most valuable of these is the back-to-front game where I tell a story with a variety of outcomes and you select the cards which best illustrate each situation. The last section leads on to the many spreads which are in use, as well as a kind of *Witch Report* on their relative values and the best way to use them. Woven into and between each segment of the book are advice sections, the largest of which outlines the benefits and pitfalls of becoming a professional Tarot Reader as well as how to go about this. (N.B. You may notice that I use *he* and *she* in a random and interchangeable manner. This is quite deliberate.)

I hope that by working through this book and trying out the ideas on your friends and colleagues at work, you will enjoy this highly original guide to Tarot reading. I also hope that you will have gone a long way to solving the seemingly impossible problem of how to string the cards together to tell a story.

Chapter 1

Useful Tips for Beginners and Improvers Alike

Absolute beginners

If you have just bought or been given your first pack of Tarot cards and don't know where to begin, read this section first. If you are a complete beginner, you will find that the booklet which accompanies your new deck of cards will give you a little basic information but you will need something far more comprehensive than this. Look around your library and local bookshop for inspiration. Go to any festivals and events in your area which might have occult books for sale and also put yourself on the mailing list of The Aquarian Press who published this book. The mailing list doesn't oblige you to buy anything, it simply means that you will be sent information from time to time. I have written a couple of books on Tarot but I suggest that you read a variety of books by different authors because everyone presents the Tarot differently and you will need a diversification of ideas.

In addition to this, look around your neighbourhood for classes, read the psychic magazines and see if there are any correspondence courses available. You might gather a few friends together and approach your local Tarot Reader to see if he or she would be willing to teach you. You will also need to go and have a reading yourself from time to time, so that you can see how it works when done by an experienced professional Reader. In the meantime, try to ensure that you become reasonably familiar with the cards and their basic meanings as a foundation for future readings.

Practical advice

Make sure that the cards which you buy have both the Major and the Minor Arcanas fully illustrated with pictures which give a clear indication of their meanings. A card which shows merely four or five swords is difficult for a beginner to understand, whereas cards which carry pictures which tell

IV FORTUNE   XI TOWER

The Merlin Tarot   The Magickal Tarot

The Arthurian Tarot   The Norse Tarot

The Prediction Tarot

The Servants of the Light Tarot   The Celtic Tarot

a story are easier to follow. There are some gifted people who prefer the plainer cards either because they are so psychic that they are not really using the cards at all, or because they are used to reading conventional playing cards. This is fair enough, but *you* probably need all the help you can get.

There are many, possibly hundreds, of Tarot packs but the following examples which have been used to illustrate this book are all published by The Aquarian Press and should be freely available. Please note that there is considerable variation in the design of Tarot packs — for example, the numbering in *The Merlin Tarot* and the names in *The Servants of the Light Tarot* — and the decks used in this book will make you more aware of this.

How to 'energize' a new deck of cards

Simply handling the cards will begin the process of energizing or charging-up; however there are other ways of doing this. The following method was shown to me many years ago by a Tarot Reader called Edward Ubels.

Take the new cards out of their packet and spread them out face upwards on a table or on the floor. Borrow an old pack of well-used Tarot cards from a very trusted friend and lay each card face downwards on its companion in the new deck. After this, ask for a blessing for the cards so that they will bring peace and healing to all those who look for their help and protection so that they won't pick up any unpleasant 'vibes' along the way. After this keep them safely in a box. Many people wrap their cards in silk to keep them protected from evil influences. I keep mine in an Italian alabaster cigarette box and I don't wrap them in anything.

Shuffling and dealing

You can give the cards to your Questioner to shuffle and then you can deal them straight off the top of the deck. Alternatively, you can ask him to cut the cards and then discard one half. He can cut them three times with the left hand, moving leftwards and then put them back together. You can even shuffle them yourself on behalf of your Questioner (this is very useful for readings which are carried out on the telephone). Try everything until you find the routine which suits you best.

How much do you need to learn?

It is not essential to learn the meanings of all the cards parrot-fashion just yet. Confine yourself to learning the Major Arcana and the underlying meaning of the four suits of the Minor Arcana without worrying yet about each individual card. Get some idea about the Court cards and, even at this early stage, begin to give some mini-readings to your friends. Remember to be flexible in your reading of the cards and accept that your interpretation of each and every card will change slightly with every reading you do.

Don't bother with the meanings of negative (reversed) cards at all for the moment. You may never use them, but you might need to look up the odd reversed meaning on occasion. As it happens, I use reversed cards quite a lot but I know that this is unusual amongst Tarot Readers.

Chapter 2

The Major Arcana

I have not provided a full explanation of each Major Arcana card in this book but only a brief 'memory jogger' comprising the key ideas and any supplementary meanings that might apply. I have also provided a brief reminder of any negative (reversed card) meanings which can be useful on those occasions when a card appears to be giving an unusual meaning. Reversals can be very handy when dealing with the Court cards because a reversed Court card immediately warns that the person to whom it refers is not as decent or reliable as the Questioner would like him to be.

This section is illustrated with cards from *The Celtic Tarot*, designed and painted by Courtney Davis.

The Fool No. 0

Key ideas The opening of a new chapter, the beginning of a real or metaphorical journey. A totally new situation of an unspecified kind which could take the Questioner anywhere. Look at the surrounding cards to see what this new beginning or journey is all about.

Supplementary meanings Nil.

Negative meanings The Questioner should look before leaping into something new because of unseen problems. He must be careful not to become obsessed with someone or something and should strive to keep a sense of proportion.

The Magician No. 1

Key ideas A new opportunity and a chance to shine. The Questioner should market himself and use the skills which he has already gained in order to impress others and to succeed. A new job or any situation which requires courage and skill.

Supplementary meanings Independence, self-reliance and self-motivation. This card frequently denotes freelance work or self-employment. Some Readers see this card as the beginning of psychic development while others feel that it is an indication that an important man is coming into their lives. (I personally see the Emperor as an important man.)

Negative meanings The Questioner may miss an opportunity through fear, lack of faith in himself or reluctance to take a chance and leave the past behind. On the other hand, he may be over-confident and unrealistic. He must watch out for trickery as things may not be all that they appear to be. New schemes should be thoroughly checked out. A negative Magician may simply denote that this is a poor time to take an 'iffy' job or to become self-employed.

The High Priestess No. 2

Key ideas Experience and wisdom combined with intuition. A cool head ruling a warm heart. Help, advice and tuition, possibly given by a woman. Something which is not yet revealed. Psychic ability.

Supplementary meanings Patience will be required as life could appear to slow down in the near future. Mental rather than physical activities will be important. There could be a diminishing of sexual activity for a while.

Negative meanings Loss of control, hysterical outbursts and an over-charged emotional atmosphere. The Questioner may be up against prejudice or he may feel prejudice towards others. A woman may be wearing herself out for her family and leaving no time for herself. Finally, the reversal of this card can suggest an improvement in the Questioner's sex-life!

The Empress No. 3

Key ideas Comfortable and beautiful surroundings. Land and gardens. A loving, motherly woman. Abundance and fruitfulness. Possibly pregnancy. Success and extra money to be spent on the home and family.

Supplementary meanings Nil.

Negative meanings There may be problems related to pregnancy. Alternatively, the Questioner may decide not to have any more children and may opt for sterilization at this time. There may be a greedy woman trying to get her hands on an unfair amount of land or property.

The Emperor No. 4

Key ideas The masculine force. A man of influence. Temporal power and status for a person of either sex. A helpful man who acts as a mentor. A strong partner or husband. Promotion and higher status for the Questioner himself.

Supplementary meanings It is worth pointing out that the Emperor is connected with *worldly* rather than spiritual power and also that he resents rivals.

Negative meanings The Questioner may have a man in her life who is not all that he makes himself out to be, possibly because he is ill or because he is a wimp in Superman's clothes! If the card represents a situation, the Questioner will find it difficult to progress, especially at work, for a while.

The Hierophant No. 5

Key ideas Tradition and conventional behaviour. Spiritual authority, a kindly advisor, a teacher or an arbitrator. Marriage.

Supplementary meanings If the Questioner is waiting for something to happen, it soon will. He may find himself in a place of worship soon, possibly attending a wedding or a similar event.

Negative meanings A marriage may not come off. The Questioner may be advised to stay single. Unconventional tactics will be better than orthodox ones at this time. The Questioner may be badly or inadequately advised by someone.

The Lovers No. 6

Key ideas Choice. The beginning of a new relationship or the re-emergence of an old one. Beauty and harmony in one's surroundings.

Supplementary meanings The Questioner may soon improve his image and his surroundings by buying new clothing or equipment. He may redecorate or refurbish his home.

Negative meanings Partings, the end of an affair. A decision which is opposed by others, especially family members. An impossible choice or even the wrong choice.

The Chariot No. 7

Key ideas Movement and change. Travel and transport. Conflict resulting in victory, triumph over adversity. The need to control opposing or conflicting forces.

Supplementary meanings Indecision, two roads to choose from.

Negative meanings The Questioner may be too busy. He may have difficulty in coping with conflicting interests around him. Travel plans may become confused and disarranged and a new vehicle may become a necessity.

Strength No. 8

Key ideas Patience, endurance, the gentle force. Good or improved health. Assertiveness. The return of confidence. Tact and diplomacy.

Supplementary meanings If the Questioner is being bullied or put-upon, he will soon be able to change this situation without becoming a bully himself.

Negative meanings There is illness around the Questioner. He may be ill himself, or have dealings with sick people. He may be depressed and unhappy. His position in life may be weak and it may be necessary to take steps to improve this.

The Hermit No. 9

Key ideas Quiet contemplation and introspection. Centering oneself or centering one's psychic energies. Wise counsel and enlightenment. Retreat, reflection and a time of patient waiting or preparation. Being alone by choice.

Supplementary meanings Nil.

Negative meanings The Questioner may not relish the idea of a quiet spell and may decline offers of help. He may refuse to grow up or to take responsibility for himself and will fear loneliness. His confidence will be at a low ebb and he may find it hard to deal with feelings of rage or jealousy, or he may be on the receiving end of someone else's jealous and unreasonable behaviour. At worst, bereavement and rejection.

The Wheel of Fortune No. 10

Key ideas What goes up must come down. Everything changes.

Supplementary meanings The element of 'Fortune' could suggest luck or money on the way.

Negative meanings A period of stagnation or even of bad luck. Not the best time for the Questioner to take a chance.

Justice No. 11

Key ideas Legal matters which produce a just result. Fairness, an apology given or received. Balance, harmony. Arbitration.

Supplementary meanings The Questioner is being urged to act in a completely honest and above-board manner and to avoid illegal or unethical situations.

Negative meanings Injustice, either in the form of unjust or unfair treatment. A legal problem or an unfair court decision.

The Hanged Man No. 12

Key ideas Suspension, a temporary state of limbo. Spiritual values versus material concerns. Sacrifice of one thing in order to have another. Initiation into a new group through shared experiences of pain and sorrow.

Supplementary meanings Nil

Negative meanings A period of indecision or suspension is coming to an end. The Questioner must guard against making useless sacrifices or making a martyr of himself.

Death No. 13

Key ideas Change, transformation. Something old giving way to something new. Sometimes this does show that someone around the Questioner will die, but it is much more likely to show a situation coming to an end.

Supplementary meanings Nil.

Negative meanings Changes might be less drastic when the card is used negatively. A loss of a friendship is possible.

Temperance No. 14

Key ideas Moderation in all things. The right mixture. Peace.

Supplementary meanings Nil.

Negative meanings Pressures and too much 'busyness'. Anxieties and an unbalanced way of life. The Questioner may not be able to compromise for the sake of others, or he may find that others refuse to compromise for him. Possible intemperance with regard to food, drink, etc.

The Devil No. 15

Key ideas Unnecessary guilt feelings. Bondage to the past or to a situation which is no longer relevant. Misplaced loyalties. Sex, lust, fear, addiction. Also a commitment which is healthy although heavy, such as a mortgage.

Supplementary meanings The Questioner must look at the practicalities of his situation in addition to considering emotional and philosophical aspects. The Questioner may develop an unhealthy attachment to something or someone.

Negative meanings A spiritual rather than a practical approach may be required. Sexual matters will improve and problems of obsession or possession will cease. A period of commitment or of being tied to a situation will come to an end. The Questioner will realize that he doesn't need to remain in a rotten situation and will extricate himself from it.

The Tower No. 16

Key ideas A shock; a collapse of plans. An awakening which brings enlightenment. A surprise, but not necessarily a disaster.

Supplementary meanings Sometimes this card signifies a problem with regard to property or business premises. There could be something wrong with the structure or the fittings and fixtures of a building.

Negative meanings This card is much the same either way up but when reversed or used negatively, it represents a surprise rather than a shock. The event could have already occurred and may already be in the process of being dealt with.

The Star No. 17

Key ideas Faith in the future, making plans. Hope, success and expansion of horizons. Education.

Supplementary meanings The gaining of occult knowledge, especially in astrology.

Negative meanings Some delay in new ventures. Difficulties in studying. Perhaps the Questioner should leave things alone for a while, and wait for a more propitious time.

The Moon No. 18

Key ideas Dreams, illusions, self-delusion and overwhelming emotion. Lies and mysteries. Muddled feelings and indecision.

Supplementary meanings There may be problems associated with the Questioner's mother or any kind of mother-figure. On a more positive note, this card denotes travel and also an increase in psychic awareness.

Negative meanings A period of confusion will come to an end soon.

The Sun No. 19

Key ideas Joy, happiness, success. Exams passed. Children may figure in the Questioner's life soon.

Supplementary meanings The summer may be important in some way. There could be a trip abroad to a sunny place.

Negative meanings The Questioner might have problems with regard to children. A female Questioner may experience difficulty in becoming pregnant. A marriage may be unsuccessful because the Questioner is not being appreciated or loved enough.

Judgement No. 20

Key ideas The end of a project and an assessment of its worth. Something which comes alive once again. Legal matters.

Supplementary meanings Good judgement may be needed soon.

Negative meanings Something is coming to an end, possibly against the Questioner's wishes. Legal matters may be disappointing in their outcome. A past situation may now be considered as having been a waste of time.

The World No. 21

Key ideas Full circle. The completion of a cycle. A new road is ahead. Travel and expansion of horizons.

Supplementary meanings Nil.

Negative meanings The Questioner may not be happy with the changes which are taking place and may resent the fact that he is being asked to cope with something new. Travel plans may be delayed. The Questioner may choose to visit familiar places rather than new ones or to remain in a rut rather than move with the times.

The Fool No. 0

Key ideas A journey, a fresh start, the beginning of an enterprise. This is the first card and also the last one. The circle is never broken, life goes on even after death.

Chapter 3

Skill Building With the Major Arcana Cards

Now is the time to get your friends together and try out a couple of experiments. Using only the Major Arcana cards, ask a friend to pick one card from the pack at random and give it to you. You should then try to apply the message on the card to her current situation. Ask her to give you some feedback on your findings. Here is an example of the technique in action.

This section is illustrated with cards from *The Merlin Tarot*, designed by R.J. Stewart and painted by Miranda Gray. (The numbers on the cards themselves do not follow the conventional order.)

No. 10 The Wheel of Fortune

You are going through a period of rapid change just now which should bring an improvement to your life in general and to your finances in particular. You will soon be able to take advantage of many different opportunities. These opportunities may be financial, social, educational or for career advancement. You are not completely in control of these changes; they are, to a great extent in the hands of fate or destiny.

IV FORTUNE

The Feedback

This card was picked at random by my daughter, Helen, who had just changed her job. She was temporarily short of money because she had bought herself a car in order to travel to this job, which seemed to offer more opportunities for advancement than any of her previous ones. It is just a thought, but I wonder if the 'wheel' on the Wheel of Fortune card represented her new form of transport?

Now go ahead and try the technique for yourself. I have asked my friend Peter to pick one for you and he chose The Lovers. I leave it up to you to work out what is happening in Peter's life just now.

Now pick one for yourself and see what you make of it, then try the same thing out on one of your friends.

XX LOVERS

Combining two cards

This is where you will find the 'key idea' section in the previous chapter useful. Please feel free to substitute or add your own key ideas. If you have difficulty in interpreting any of the cards, look at the supplementary and negative sections in the previous chapter for added inspiration. If two cards just don't appear to blend together however much you try to make them do so, then use the first card to indicate a past situation and try the second one as an indication of future events.

Here are a couple which I have worked out for you but please look at them yourself and make up *your own* interpretation of the situation.

No. 8 Strength

Patience, endurance. The gentle force. Good or improved health. Assertiveness. The return of confidence. Tact and diplomacy.

No. 9 The Hermit

Quiet contemplation and introspection. Centering oneself. Wise counsel and enlightenment. Retreat, reflection and a time of patient waiting or preparation. Being alone by choice.

XVIII STRENGTH

XIV HERMIT

No. 8 Strength and No. 9 The Hermit

The Questioner may be enjoying a calm spell which will promote her mental, physical, spiritual and emotional well-being. A calm, tactful and wise approach to problems should be sought. Quiet study is recommended at this time rather than action. My own instinct and intuition as a Tarot Reader would be to tell the Questioner to seek sensible advice and to keep a few things to herself, also to enjoy the period of retreat and reflection which is being imposed upon her.

The following pair of cards don't seem to have anything in common, but they do have a link with each other via the opposite ideas of *freedom* versus *bondage*.

No. 15 The Devil

Unnecessary guilt feelings. Bondage to the past or to a situation which is no longer relevant. Misplaced loyalties. Sex, lust, fear, addiction. Also a healthy commitment such as a mortgage.

No. 7 The Chariot

Movement and change. Travel and transport. Conflict resulting in victory and triumph over adversity. The need to control opposing or conflicting forces (also indecision).

X GUARDIAN

IX CHARIOT

No. 15 The Devil and No. 7 The Chariot

The combination of these two cards would suggest to me that the Questioner is facing a choice between staying put and trying to alter an obviously unsatisfactory situation or getting out of it altogether. (However, remember that Tarot interpretation is an intensely personal thing, and if you feel differently about these two cards, please follow your own instincts because they are never wrong.)

My interpretation of the combination of these two cards would be that the issue of freedom and bondage is the common factor. The other factors of sex, addiction, lust and spiritual enlightenment (The Devil), and of travel and transport (The Chariot), don't seem to me to fit together at all. The supplementary idea of indecision *does* fit, however, because any situation which revolves around freedom versus bondage requires difficult decisions to be made by the Questioner. In a full reading, the surrounding Minor Arcana cards would supply the reasons for the bondage and the means of obtaining freedom.

Here is a two-card combination for you to work out for yourself. This one is easy because there is an obvious link between them. I have even hinted at the connection by emphasizing the common key-idea words.

No. 2 The Priestess   No. 17 The Star

Experience and wisdom combined with intuition. A cool head ruling a warm heart. *Help, advice, tuition,* possibly given by a woman. Something which is not yet revealed. Psychic ability.

Faith in the future, making plans. Hope, success and expansion of horizons. *Education.*

XXI PRIESTESS

III STAR

Here are some more combinations which I have picked out at random for you to work on:

XVI TEMPERANCE

IV FORTUNE

No. 16 Temperance and No. 10 The Wheel of Fortune

Peace versus upheavals perhaps, or moderation versus excess or spirituality versus practicality or boredom versus excitement. See what you think about the combination of these two cards.

VI JUDGEMENT

XIX EMPRESS

No. 20 Judgement and No. 3 The Empress

A situation which has come to a fruitful conclusion. I think this is an apt point upon which to close this chapter of my book!

Chapter 4

The Minor Arcana —
The Elements

The four suits and the elements

Each of the four suits of the Minor Arcana has its own personality and these are often allied to the ancient idea of the four elements of Earth, Water, Fire and Air. Astrologers are accustomed to using these elements in their work but if they try to make them work in exactly the same way in Tarot as they do in astrology, they will find themselves becoming very confused. The elements of Earth and Water work in a similar way in both systems but while the element of Fire has some similarities, the element of Air is used quite differently.

The suits, here referred to as Pentacles, Cups, Wands and Swords, often have different names in the various Tarot decks — Pentacles might be Coins, Disks or Spheres, for example — and you will therefore have to bear this in mind when working with your chosen deck.

The suit of Pentacles and the element of Earth

Pentacles are associated with *resources* and *values*. The Earth element refers to the material world, things which can be seen, heard, felt and counted. Therefore, in practical terms, this may be the Questioner's bank account, his land, property, business, possessions, valuable goods or anything else which he values. This suit rules money, work which produces money, earnings, savings and outgoings. It also relates to security, growth and progress, especially in the sense of practical, material growth which can be seen and measured. The accountancy side of a business is a Pentacle matter, as are the profit or loss situations. Status, importance and the value of goods or of people is assessed by this suit.

People who are represented by this suit are practical and business-like, reliable and resourceful, but possibly a little dull. (NB. A pentacle, or five-pointed star, represents all the elements of Earth, Water, Fire and Air, in addition to the element of Spirituality.)

The suit of Cups and the element of Water

Cups are associated with both *emotion* and *feelings*, also *love* and *comfort*. The water/feelings element may be expressed in the usual areas of love and relating, such as the general patterns of love which exist within a family or the more powerful emotion of falling in love. The Cups also refer to friendship, companionship and pleasant colleagues as well as to comfortable living and working surroundings. This suit may refer to artistic or creative development and the kind of education or training which either brings out the Questioner's creativity or makes him feel better about himself and the things he is trying to achieve. This suit also shows how the Questioner feels about any situation in which he finds himself. For example, he may choose to stay in a job which pays badly but in which he feels happy and fulfilled. As you can see from this example, it is the *emotional* response to any situation which is revealed by this suit.

People who are represented by this suit are kind, friendly, caring and creative, but possibly lacking in positiveness.

The suit of Wands and the element of Fire

The Wand cards are concerned with *day-to-day matters* and also the *energy* and *enthusiasm* to make things happen. They are associated with communications in the form of letters and phone calls and local and more distant travel as well as the kind of tasks we all perform every day at work and at home. The Wands can show whether these matters will go smoothly or whether the Questioner will suffer frustration, delays and obstacles to his efforts. This suit also refers to property and premises, but in respect of their suitability, convenience and the opportunities which these present rather than their monetary value. The fire element denotes energy and enterprise, creativity and the urge to get things off the ground. Business concerns, creative enterprises and negotiations of all kinds are Wand matters.

The people who are represented by this suit are cheerful, outgoing, fun-loving and enthusiastic, but they can be shallow.

The suit of Swords and the element of Air

The Swords are concerned with a number of different things. They rule the realm of the mind both in the form of *ideas* and *worries* and also relate to serious decisions, delays, disappointments, restrictions, losses and separations. Secondly, they rule matters which need the services of a *specialist* or a *professional person*, such as a doctor, policeman, solicitor or other special advisor. Lastly, the Swords are associated with travel and movement, either literal travel in the form of physical journeys or metaphorical travel in the form of moving on in some way and instigating ideas and new beginnings. The easiest way to think of this suit is in terms of its connection with difficult decisions or problems which demand attention. Travel, rest and recuperation are also part of this suit because it seems to carry within it the contradictions of ill-health versus recovery, restriction versus movement and over-work versus rest. I guess the easiest way to understand this suit is to remember that it is associated with mental activity.

People who are represented by this suit are strong-minded, intellectual, and good at leading others, but they may be too serious or a little withdrawn or aggressive.

An example which might help you remember

1. *The idea* The Swords will precipate a decision. An example of this might be a change in the atmosphere at the Questioner's place of work, where a previously happy situation has vanished and been replaced by an unacceptable level of aggravation.
2. *The activity* The Wands provide the enthusiasm and energy for the search for a new job. They suggest arrangements for an interview and the courage to go through with it.
3. *The result* The Pentacles denote that the new job pays well and also offers opportunities for training and advancement.
4. The Cups show that the Questioner will enjoy the 'job satisfaction' that this new work offers. This satisfaction can only be measured on an emotional level and may or may not be influenced by the increased income and opportunities which the new job offers.

Another memory jogger

Pentacles equal material resources.
Cups equal emotional responses.
Wands equal day-to-day achievements/hold-ups.
Swords equal ideas/worries, problems/solutions.

The Court cards

We will take a close look at the Court cards a little later on, but just for the time being, when a Court card appears in a reading, look at it in the following rather simplistic terms: if the Court card is a King, the person will be a mature man; if a Queen, a mature woman; a Knight represents a young person (usually male); the Page is either a young woman or a child.

Skill building with the Minor Arcana cards only

Now find a couple of willing guinea-pigs and ask them to take five or six cards from the pack at random. Remove any Major Arcana cards and see what the suits of the Minor Arcana cards can tell you about them. Look at the following two examples before trying this for yourself.

Mainly Pentacles but with a Cup and a Wand card as well

This person has some minor practical problems on his mind; he may be worried about money, property or his position in life. He feels fairly good about his situation but he will soon have to muster the energy to make any necessary adjustments to his life.

Mainly Cups with one Sword card

This person has a major decision to make about a relationship. He will have to examine his feelings and possibly also those of others. The problem cannot be dodged, and the only way he is going to be able to put things right is by acting decisively.

Skill-building sessions

Now it's *your* turn. Follow the instructions and see how you get on. First, select five cards and discard any Major Arcana cards:

Now look at the number of cards in each suit:

Mainly Pentacles	yes/no
Mainly Cups	yes/no
Mainly Wands	yes/no
Mainly Swords	yes/no

Now try to blend them remembering which suits represent difficult decisions, love and relating, communicating or material matters.

Chapter 5

Skill Building
With the Whole Pack

This section is the most important part of this book because if you get the hang of this, you will have overcome most of your problems. Have faith in yourself because it's not as hard as you think; just read through the hints, explanations and instructions and work through the suggested exercises and you will soon have it 'cracked'! You will need to use the whole pack of cards with the Major and the Minor Arcana cards all mixed up together.

The following points will be very helpful to you.

1. Don't try to predict the future at this stage. Concentrate on picking up the Questioner's *present* situation. If the reading begins to drift into the future as you go along that's great, but don't aim for it. Check your findings after the reading by asking your Questioner for some feedback.
2. Use your imagination. You may feel on occasion that you are simply making up a fairy story rather than giving a reading but don't be put off by this feeling as you will find to your surprise that your 'story' will ring true to your Questioner.
3. If you find yourself experiencing any kind of clairvoyant or psychic happening as you go along, don't try to fight it but allow it to happen. You may literally 'see' a situation in your mind's eye or you may get a strong impression about something which is occurring in the Questioner's life. When this happens just go with the flow and allow anything which you feel, see or hear in your head to come out and be acknowledged. Any feedback which the Questioner gives you after the reading will almost certainly confirm that your feelings etc. were right. Don't be inhibited by the thought of looking foolish; you may find yourself completely wrong on occasion but more often than not you will be right. This is one of the arguments in favour of learning and practising in a group where you can all help and encourage each other.

Incidentally, even if you don't consider that you are using any psychic abilities, you probably *are* doing so without realizing it, therefore I suggest that right from the start you get into the habit of 'closing down' after each Tarot session. If you understand psychic techniques and are already using a method of closing which works for you then please continue. If you are new to the idea of closing down the easiest way to do this is to imagine yourself stepping into a sleeping-bag and zipping it up around you and even over your head. This will protect you and your aura from unwanted 'vibes'. A good shower or bath is also recommended but you can save this until a bit later in the day when it is more convenient. Professional psychics are the cleanest people on earth because they are always washing themselves.

4. Remember that *your* definition of any card is always the right one. You may begin to deviate from the 'standard' Tarot interpretations as your readings progress. If a particular card or a cumulation of cards begins to mean something different to you than it does to everyone else, that is a good thing.

The four-card trick

The following technique is astoundingly simple. Get together with your fellow Tarot students, or if there is nobody else around who is interested in learning the Tarot persuade some friends to join in and help you.

Ask your first Questioner to shuffle the pack a little and to choose four cards at random. Then proceed as follows:

1. Lay all four cards out in a row in the upright position. (Don't even *think* about using reversed cards at this stage.)
2. Take a look at the cards and assess the number of cards in each of the following categories:

    (a) Major Arcana cards
    (b) Cup cards
    (c) Wand cards
    (d) Sword cards
    (e) Pentacle cards
    (f) Court cards

    Some of the cards will fall into two categories, for instance the King of Cups is both a *Cup* card and a *Court* card.
3. If you pick four cards at random from a Tarot pack the chances are that you will end up with one Major Arcana card and three Minor Arcana ones. The second most likely situation is two Major and two Minor.

This is because there are twenty-two Major and fifty-six Minor Arcana cards in a pack.

Your next step is to look at any Major Arcana cards which have been chosen and analyse them. This will give you the 'flavour' of the reading. It will show you, for instance, whether the Questioner is happy or unhappy, going up in the world or going down, or whether her situation is stable or unstable. It will not tell you *why* she is unhappy, unstable and so on but the Minor Arcana cards will fill in those details.

4. Now look at the Minor Arcana cards and take a closer look at your Questioner's life in view of the additional information which these provide. If you are really short of an answer at this stage try muttering the following to yourself: 'Pentacles denote resources and results, Cups denote feelings, Wands denote day-to-day activities, Swords denote powerful ideas and worries while court cards denote people.'
5. Don't worry about the meanings of individual Minor Arcana cards at this stage.

Simple Sample Readings

This section is illustrated with cards from *The Magickal Tarot*, designed and painted by Anthony Clark.

Random, four-card reading no 1

| No. 19 The Sun | Three of Swords | No. 0 The Fool | Seven of Cups |

The first step is to find any connection between any of the cards. In this case, there are two Major Arcana cards and two numbered Minor Arcana cards.

Now look at the two Major cards and try to find the 'flavour' of the reading. According to the key ideas section in Chapter 2, The Sun represents joy, happiness, success and/or children; while The Fool represents a journey, a fresh start and/or the beginning of an enterprise. Therefore, you as a Tarot Reader could arrive at any of the following conclusions (and probably one or two more of your own as well):

1. A journey which will bring happiness.
2. A successful new enterprise.
3. Success and joy for the Questioner's children.
4. The birth of a child in the family.

Another way of reading these two cards is to read them from left to right (most people take to this method of reading without being prompted as it seems natural to do so).

5. In this case, the Questioner could be leaving a position of happiness, success and comfort in order to try something new. It could, alternatively, suggest that the good times are passing away now and that something which may be better or worse, but which will certainly be different, is on the way.

Now let us look at the Minor Arcana cards and see which suits are represented.

6. A Sword card and a Cup card suggest that some powerful decisions will be required which may bring worry which may play on the emotions of the Questioner. He or she will also have to take feelings (his or her own and those of others) into consideration.

Random, four-card reading no 2

(Here we see how some Tarot packs use different terminology for their cards: in *The Magickal Tarot*, Knights become Princes, Pages Princesses, and in the Major Arcana Justice is called Adjustment.)

First look at your ratios and groupings. In this case, there is one Major Arcana card which, being alone, is very powerful. There are two Court cards, which may or may not represent people, and there is one numbered Cup card.

Let us look at the Major Arcana card first. The key ideas are: legal matters

| The Knight of Swords | The Page of Pentacles | No. 11 Justice | Six of Cups |

which produce a just result; fairness; an apology given or received, also a restoration of balance and harmony. Therefore, we now know that the reading is about a real or supposed injustice of some kind.

The two Court cards suggest that other people are involved in this situation. The Knight (or Prince) of Swords card might represent a skilled and knowledgeable advisor, possibly even a professional lawyer of some kind, but it could just as well suggest strife and problems coming from an aggressive person. The Page of Pentacles (Princess of Disks) suggests that the injustice is about money or some other kind of resource, or that someone may be behaving unfairly about money or resources. The Six of Cups shows that there is quite a lot of emotion being generated here.

Now try out some more four-card readings for your friends.

Chapter 6

The Court Cards

Most people have difficulty with these cards which is why I am devoting a whole chapter to them. (You will also find a brief interpretation of the Court cards in the Minor Arcana chapter.) The best way to deal with these cards is to categorize them as follows:

Pentacles   Practical, money-minded people who are reliable, decent, good in business but also dull, materialistic and selfish. They are associated with the element of earth.

Cups   Kindly, emotional, creative people who make good friends but may be weak or unreliable as partners. They are associated with the element of water.

Wands   Active, enthusiastic, sporty, cheerful, friendly, intelligent people who are good communicators. These people make excellent businessmen and women, teachers and sales-people but they are restless and may not always tell the truth. They are associated with the element of fire.

Swords   Strong, determined, intelligent individuals who make good military leaders and professional people but who may be aggressive, spiteful or unable to put themselves into other people's shoes. They are associated with the element of air.

Kings   Mature adult men. Sometimes a young man who is very grown up in his attitudes. This person is important to the Questioner at the time of the reading.

Queens   Mature adult women. Also a young woman who is mature in her attitudes. This person is important to the Questioner at the time of the reading.

Knights	Young men, occasionally young women or a mature person who is not of vital importance to the Questioner at the time of the reading. These cards can also represent situations.
Pages	Children, young people and young women. This may be a person who is not particularly important to the Questioner at the time of the reading. These cards often represent situations.

Some Tarot Readers relate the Court cards to hair colouring as a means of identification, thus seeing the Pentacle cards as people with grey or dark hair, the Sword cards very dark hair, the Wands brown or reddish hair and the Cup cards fair hair.

I tend to use characteristics to describe each card. I can only pass on *my own* ideas as to the character of each card which may help you at this stage, but you must find your own interpretation of the personalities that these cards represent and make up your own designations for your use.

I have given you the good and bad aspects of each card together, but if you wish you can use upright cards to show the positive side of the card's nature and reversed cards to show the negative side.

This section is illustrated with cards from *The Prediction Tarot*, designed by Bernard Stringer and painted by Peter Richardson; in this deck the Pentacles are called Coins and the Wands are Staves.

The King of Pentacles

This is the kind of man who can be relied upon to do the right thing at all times. If he says he is working late at the office, that is *exactly* what he is doing. He digs the garden and washes the family car at weekends and he is a conscientious and protective family man. If he won the pools he would tuck his winnings safely away in a building society. Some people may consider him dull and he could be mean and over-materialistic. He could also be temporarily down on his luck. This chap may be into farming or land and property development. He may actually be the Questioner's bank manager or accountant or the manager of the financial department of her firm or organization.

KING OF COINS

The King of Cups

This man is kind, pleasant, warm-hearted, friendly and fond of romance. His advice is worth listening to but he may be too lazy to give much practical help. Artistic and creative, he doesn't measure the value of anything by money alone but he makes sure that he, himself, has all that he needs or wants. He is a loving family man whose happy, humorous nature makes him nice to live with but he could be weak and silly. Sometimes this card is an indication that a man in whom the Questioner is interested would be happy to offer her friendship, but not a fully-fledged relationship.

The King of Wands

This man is a good communicator and may work in sales, teaching or journalism. He is very helpful in a working environment but possibly reluctant to commit himself to an emotional partnership. He is great fun to be with and is full of enthusiasm for life. He could be a highly successful negotiator, a glamorous figure who travels and mixes with interesting people. He may be something of a 'con man' and a bit forgetful when it comes to duty and responsibility.

The King of Swords

This man is clever, serious and intellectual in outlook. He may have a career in one of the professions. His personality is strong and he is, generally speaking, quite dependable both in business and personal relationships. His judgement is good and his knowledge extensive which makes him an excellent advisor. He may be a tough, determined rather bullying type who could, in the long run, turn out to be too selfish and aggressive to live with. Alternatively, he may be withdrawn, sarcastic or even rather big-headed with an inflated opinion of himself.

Queen of Pentacles

This lady is practical, reliable and conscientious. She is very caring towards her family but may be a bit undemonstrative. She is a sensible and capable businesswoman, possibly involved with work with land, property or gardens. She needs material comforts, and will fight hard for her share of the family wealth in the event of any kind of dispute. If a woman is being 'difficult' over money, perhaps in a divorce situation, this card would turn up (reversed) in the reading.

Queen of Cups

This lady is soft and gentle, loving and caring or she may be lazy and selfish. She is artistic and will create a beautiful home and garden for herself and her family. She needs to be kept in comfort and not required to work too hard. She loves her children and is a good and loving companion. This card may well indicate that the Questioner will soon have a very good friend who really listens to her problems.

Queen of Wands

This lady is businesslike, highly-sexed and warm-hearted. She may be too busy and too temperamental for some tastes. Her career is important to her and she may take on the major financial responsibility for the family. This card turns up when the Questioner would be advised to adopt a very businesslike approach to life.

Queen of Swords

This lady is clever and competent but may be a bit too cool-hearted for some tastes. Her emotions are strong when they are aroused and she never forgives and forgets. She needs a meaningful career in order to be fulfilled. This lady can be immensely helpful to the Questioner or, conversely, a real bitch.

The Knights

The Knights are traditionally supposed to be young men, although Tarot Readers often see these cards as representing young people of both sexes. Another very common meaning is of a mature man who is less important to the Questioner than a king would be. He may be a colleague or a friend. Sometimes a knight card which follows a king of the same suit in a reading suggests that a man is decreasing in importance to the Questioner, while a knight which is followed by a king suggests that a man is increasing in importance. Remember that the knights often represent *situations* rather than people.

The following is the traditional way of looking at the knights both as persons and as situations.

Knight of Pentacles

A cautious, materialistic young man. He is reliable, dependable and rather serious but possibly a bit dull. A business matter could take off now, or there could be some travel in connection with business. The Questioner could develop an interest in land, farming or money-management.

Knight of Cups

A kindly, friendly young man. He is artistic, romantic and loving but possibly somewhat weak or unreliable. The Questioner will make some new friends soon, and she may travel in connection with friends.

Knight of Wands

A cheerful, busy young man who travels in connection with his work. He is great fun but could also be a bit of a liar. This card might indicate travel in connection with work, and it can also denote an important visitor from afar.

Knight of Swords

This may represent a clever, intellectual ambitious young man. Alternatively, this card could suggest an aggressive and slightly crazy guy who invites trouble. The Questioner may soon need to deal with people from the legal, medical or other professions. The card might indicate the arrival of a man who brings trouble, or possibly excitement, into the life of the Questioner.

The Pages

These can be children and young people of both sexes. Alternatively, they can show either the first glimmerings of a potential relationship, or the very end of one as the person in question fades away out of the Questioner's life. Remember that these minor Court cards often denote situations as well as people.

If the page appears to be negative (probably reversed) in a reading, the effects could be: (a) a child who is ill or in trouble; (b) a child who causes trouble for others or who appears to stand in the way of the Questioner's happiness; (c) a child who is being used as an excuse or an obstacle or who is being bounced back and forth between the parents.

Page of Pentacles

A quiet, reflective, rather materialistic and serious child who is old for his or her age. A small raise in salary or a small matter concerning money, goods or resources. The beginning of a relationship with a steady type of man.

Page of Cups

A sensitive, gentle, loving child who may be artistic or creative. The beginning of a course of study or some kind of job training. A new situation which turns out well. A new friendship, possibly the beginning of a romance.

Page of Wands

A lively, cheerful child who can be a bit scatter-brained. A significant letter, phone call or other form of communication. Beginning of a friendship or romance. Would benefit from writing or broadcasting something.

Page of Swords

A clever, serious child who is slightly withdrawn. Possibly a strange or even aggressive child. A contract or document of importance. Someone who warns the Questioner about something. The beginning of legal, medical or other professional help.

Points to consider when reading the Court cards

If you use cards in both their reversed and their upright positions, you will find that a person represented by a Court card which is reversed in a reading is not being particularly helpful to the Questioner. (See page 105 for more information on reversed cards.)

A final and most important point is that all readings are *subjective* and this subjectivity is two-fold. First of all, you have your own prejudices which cannot help being brought into a reading; and secondly, you have the Questioner's point of view to cope with. I have explained both of these concepts more fully in the advice chapter on page 107. As far as the Court cards are concerned, the Questioner's point of view must *always* be taken into account. For example, if your Questioner is in love with a married man with whom she wants to live, she will see his wife as an obstacle to her happiness. This is fair enough, but she may also see the wife as an evil bitch. This view of the wife would be expressed by a card such as the reversed Queen of Swords. While it is possible that this wife may indeed *be* an absolute bitch, she may just as possibly *not* be so but will be perceived by the Questioner as such simply because she stands between the Questioner and what she wants (i.e. the husband). If, a week or so after giving this reading, you had the immense bad luck to find yourself reading for the wife, you might find that she, in turn, sees the *mistress* as an interfering, thieving bitch. The fact of the matter may be that neither of these women is evil or bitchy, but that both are being played for suckers by a greedy, amoral man. The facts of the matter may be even more surreal than any of these scenarios, but you are only in a position to see the situation from the Questioner's point of view at the time of the reading; that is, *subjectively*.

Chapter 7

The Minor Arcana

Each of these cards carries a specific meaning or a key idea within itself. Some cards include subsidiary meanings in addition to the main interpretation and, in these cases, you will find that the main meaning is mentioned first, with any secondary ones following on after it. In most cases, I will try to expand the interpretations a little in order to show you some of the possible shades of meaning within the cards but you must be flexible in your approach and adapt each card to each and every reading as you see fit. Remember to refer back to Chapter 6 if you need a fuller description of the Court cards.

Some cards have good and bad sides to them and in these cases I have given you both aspects. Normally, I take both the positive and negative sides of a card into consideration when giving a reading, but you may wish to take special note of the cards in upright and reversed positions in order to differentiate between the positive and negative modes.

This section is illustrated with cards from *The Norse Tarot*, designed and painted by Clive Barrett. Note the change from Page and Knight to Prince and Princess in this pack.

The suit of Pentacles

Ace   A significant improvement in the Questioner's financial standing. A win, windfall, a raise in salary or a large payment is on the way. There is nothing negative about this card, but if it is reversed, the payment may be minimal or delayed.

Two   Juggling with money, borrowing from Peter to pay Paul. Spreading resources of time, money or energy very thinly. Sometimes this card indicates the breakup of a partnership and the subsequent splitting of resources.

Three   Being given an opportunity to earn money. A move of house or improvement to property.

Four   Security is on the way. This probably refers to financial security, but if the reading does not appear to be about money, the idea of security will have to be applied in a different way. A greedy over-materialistic attitude is possible. The negative side of this card is a lack of financial and/or other kinds of security, also exam failures and delays in a variety of projects.

Five   The Questioner may suffer a financial loss or simply be over-extended. He may feel left out of things, or simply be looking for financial or emotional support in the wrong place. Short-term love-affairs will go well, but they shouldn't be expected to last.

Six   The Questioner will soon be in a position to spend money and to pay off any out-standing debts. This may be the share out which follows a separation. Favours can now be repaid and any emotional debts cleared for good. This card also denotes acts of charity.

Seven   Slow growth, long-term advancement. Things will come to fruition eventually, although the benefits may not be entirely in terms of money. Hard work which eventually brings results. Negatively, the Questioner will not get anywhere fast just yet and will have to be patient. Also the result of years of hard work.

Eight   A new job or a promotion. A good use of skills. Negatively, the loss of a job.

Nine   Money and success are on the way. The Questioner will improve his property and land. Pleasure from outdoor activities. Often an indication of clearing out worn-out stuff in preparation for buying carpets and furniture for the home.

Ten   Money, success and pleasure from achievement. Security, happiness, family life and good friends will surround the Questioner. A forthcoming marriage will go well, but money and business could be a part of it. Travel in connection with business will go well. A pension or salary rise could be on the way.

Page   A practical, orderly, rather introverted child who prefers books and quiet games to noise and mess. A good scholar. As a situation, this would indicate a small improvement in finances, resources and status.

Knight   A man who is sensible, practical and dependable. He may be good with money or the development of land and its products. He could be mean and greedy, stodgy and dull. As a situation this would imply an improvement in the Questioner's financial position and also some travel or movement in connection with money and business.

Queen   This lady is practical, capable, reliable and conscientious. She is a steady and clever businesswoman who will fight quite hard for her rights in any dispute. She could be too determined and rather implacable, especially where money is concerned. As a situation, this would suggest a more practical approach to material matters.

King   This man is reliable and conscientious; he is a good businessman and could make good use of land and the resources which come from it. He may be mean, too materialistic, and rather a dull companion, but he offers a kind of security. As a situation, this would imply a practical approach to resources and a successful outcome to business matters.

The Suit of Cups

Ace   The beginning of a good friendship or work association. Love and affection, romance and marriage could be on the way. A gift, even a ring, may be received. Good social life. If reversed or a negative mood, this card implies friendship rather than love or the ending of a love affair.

Two   A loving partnership, possibly an engagement. Good colleagues and a happy atmosphere at work. Negatively, a parting.

Three   Joy, celebrations of all kinds. The Questioner may be going to a wedding. If this card appears for no apparent reason, it shows that the reading concerns the Questioner's marital status. Because this card is connected to marriages it can also imply divorce.

Four   Dissatisfaction. The grass seems to be
              greener over the hill. The Questioner has
              a lot to be grateful for, but is still missing
              something. When reversed or negative,
              this card represents new friends and
              something new to look forward to.

Five   Loss and sadness, even a period of
              mourning. However all is not lost and the
              Questioner will soon be able to re-build his
              life.

Six   Back to the future! The Questioner may
              renew an old association or possibly
              attend a family gathering and catch up
              with all the gossip. Old skills will have to be
              resurrected for use in the future. It is
              possible that some aspect of the past, even
              of the Questioner's childhood, will have to
              be re-examined and put into perspective.
              Children may soon become important in
              some way.

Seven   Muddle and confusion with too many
              options to choose from. It might be better
              to leave any major decisions for another
              time. If money is holding up a romance,
              this will soon be put right.

Eight   The Questioner will turn her back on an unsatisfactory or messy situation soon. Bad times will continue for a while but patience will bring its rewards. Tradition has it that when this card appears, a blonde woman will turn out to be helpful to the Questioner. The negative or reversed aspect of this card is that a bad time is at an end and that the Questioner will soon be attending a celebration.

Nine   Satisfaction and pleasure are on the way, but the Questioner will have to guard against smugness. Marriage to a mature person may be indicated. If a project has not worked out satisfactorily, the Questioner should try again soon.

Ten   Joy, happiness and prosperity. Family life will go well. Negatively, there may be a temporary blight on family life or the Questioner might find that his children are leaving home to become independent.

Page   A gentle, loving, artistic child. A new situation which turns out well. Anything to do with training, education or even teaching. The beginning of a friendship or a relationship which is fading away.

Knight   A kindly, friendly rather romantic young man who may be a little weak. The Questioner will make some new friends soon and he may travel in connection with friends.

Queen   Gentle, sensuous, caring, earth-mother type of woman. She is a good homemaker, a kind friend and a good listener. Alternatively, the lazy and materialistic kind of woman who spends her day watching television and eating chocolates.

King   A kind, pleasant, friendly, warm-hearted man who is very romantic. He could be a good friend and a good listener, an excellent advisor, but he may also be lazy, materialistic, weak and selfish.

The suit of Wands

Ace   The birth of an enterprise, in some cases the birth of a child. An important letter, especially in connection with a business matter. Good news. The start of something good.

Two   Partnerships matters, enterprises which involve at least one other person. A move of house or business premises. Dealing with a proud man. Negatively, there may be a partnership which works out badly or breaks up after a period of time.

Delays in buying or selling property or premises, or problems in business partnerships. This may be a bad time for negotiations; there could be bad news on the way. A proud man may cause difficulties.

Three   A new project, new job or new beginning. Travel in connection with work, negotiations or news regarding business or work matters. Marriages and partnerships will go well in future.

Four   A move of house or the purchase of premises. The Questioner will put down roots and make himself comfortable in a new area. A creative enterprise will go well. Negatively speaking, there may be problems with regard to property.

Five   The Questioner will accept a challenge which calls for patience and courage, but he will be able to win through in the end. Travel plans may be delayed or there may be legal problems.

Six   Victory, achievement. Legal, business and other problems will soon be solved. Agreements will be reached.

Seven   Opposition and possibly health problems. However, if the Questioner tackles his problems one at a time, he will be able to cope. An embarrassing situation may arise.

Eight   The Questioner can expect to travel, make new friends and enjoy some new mind-broadening experiences. Friendship or even love may be on the way. (N.B. If the Questioner wants to know *where* he is going to be travelling, this card would suggest a hot country.) Negatively speaking, there may be cancelled plans, delays through strike action and transport problems, especially in relation to public transport. Jealousy and spite are around the Questioner now.

Nine   The Questioner is on firm ground but he may have one more small problem to tackle. The best thing to do now is to leave well alone. Negatively speaking, there may be danger and loss and the Questioner's status could be undermined. Illness could be on the way.

Ten   Burdens and responsibilities are on the way. Depending upon circumstances, this could ultimately improve the Questioner's status and situation or it could just mean a lot of work for nothing much in return.

Page   A lively, intelligent but scatterbrained and restless child. An important letter or phone call. The beginning of friendship or romance. Also writing for money.

Knight   A cheerful, busy young man who travels in connection with business. He may be a good negotiator and great fun but also something of a liar. There may be travel in connection with work or an important visitor from far away.

Queen   This lady is highly-sexed, warm-hearted and a good businesswoman. She may be too temperamental or too assertive for some tastes but she is great company and good fun when in a relaxed mood. A more businesslike approach to life will soon be needed.

King   A good communicator who may work in teaching, sales or journalism and who may be helpful in a working environment but possibly evading commitments in personal life. A successful negotiator; an enterprising man who mixes with interesting people. However, he could be rather devious and a bit of a liar.

The suit of Swords

Ace A new idea, also a sense of power being placed in the Questioner's hands. If the Questioner is ill, this would indicate surgery, medical investigations and injections soon. The Questioner may over-react or may start throwing his weight about soon.

Two Stalemate, delay, nothing changing yet. This may also indicate an agreement or a settlement of some kind. If reversed this card means change and movement.

Three Loss, separation or heartache. Illness and operations, especially to do with the heart and the blood supply. Negatively or re-versed, this suggests the end of a time of loss and heartache. The beginning of emotional and physical recovery. Minor surgical procedures, possibly dental or other similar treatment. Death and fu-nerals are possible.

Four   The standard meaning of this card is that the Questioner will soon be able to have a rest or a period of time away from work and chores. However, I find that the Four of Swords often appears when the Questioner is going to be involved with hospitals in some way, either because she herself is going to be ill, or because someone around her becomes ill. There could be a joyful visit to a doctor or hospital because a baby is on the way, but I have also seen this appear in circumstances where someone *works* in a hospital or is moving house to *live* near one. This is one of those cases where you will have to work out whether the standard meaning (rest and recuperation) is the right one for you, or the rest and/or hospital connection is more appropriate.

Five   Arguments, violence, battles and things generally coming to a head. Ruined plans, losses and even heartbreak. The receiving end of spite and jealousy. People around the Questioner may suddenly become hostile for no particular reason or he may have to deal with people displaying what Americans call an 'attitude problem'. Traditionally speaking, this card also indicates a funeral.

Six   Travel overseas, a journey of importance or possibly a metaphorical move away from troubles. There may be an overseas visitor soon. Negatively speaking, delays.

Seven   There seem to be two meanings to this card. The first is of a move onwards, leaving a part of one's life behind which is either sacrificed as part of the move forward, or which needs to be left behind. The second meaning is of a robbery or a rip-off. In either case, the Questioner may need legal or insurance advice. He may also be undermining or putting something over on others.

Eight   The Questioner will be stuck in a difficult situation for a while; a typical situation would be that of a young woman left on her own with small children. Hard times surround the Questioner. Someone may be in trouble with the law. There may be disappointments, accidents or even deaths to be coped with. However the restrictions and the run of bad luck will pass away soon.

Nine   This is another of those cards where, for me at least, the 'standard' meaning is not enough. The standard meaning is of worry and sleepless nights. However, I have found this to denote problems with regard to females in the family and also to 'female' health problems. The Questioner may be on the receiving end of spite and slander.

Ten   Treachery, a stab in the back. This may indicate the total ending of a situation in much the same way that the Death card in the Major Arcana does. It may signify a forced change which is not by choice. This card can also be interpreted in connection with health matters, and in this case it suggests injections and medical investigations.

Page   A child who is clever and serious or, conversely, one who is aggressive and not quite sane. A contract or document of importance. The beginning of legal, medical or other professional help. There may be someone who keeps the Questioner informed, looks out for him and keeps him *wise* to whatever is going on behind his back or out of his sight.

Knight   A clever, intellectual, ambitious young man or, alternatively, an aggressive person who is slightly unbalanced. Possibly, the arrival of a man who brings trouble with him. There could be dealings with legal, medical or other professional people.

Queen   A clever and competent lady who is cool and collected. Alternatively a real bitch. Legal, professional and medical people may be needed soon.

King   A clever, serious, intellectual man whose judgement is excellent. He could, alternatively, be a sarcastic aggressive bully or a big-head who is impossible to live with.

Chapter 8

Practice Readings With the Whole Pack

The four-card trick

The method is to take four cards and then consider the *combinations* which arise. This can be done with any number of cards, but I suggest that you stick to four cards at this stage because this will be enough to provide variety but not enough to muddle you.

Combinations

Now look at your four cards. Leave them in the position in which they turned up but mentally work through the little list below.

1. Are there any Major Arcana cards? What are they?
2. Mentally group any Court cards together.
3. See which suits are represented.
4. See if there are two cards with the same number, e.g. two Fives.
5. Begin to think about the 'flavour' of the reading. Is it about change or stasis, inner confusion or certainty, advice, money, sex, love, the home, the job, travel and transport or what?

An example

This section is illustrated with cards from *The Arthurian Tarot*, devised by Caitlín and John Matthews and painted by Miranda Gray. Many of the cards have deliberately Arthurian names, but their traditional counterparts are given under each card for clarification.

I asked my son's business partner, Simon, to choose four cards at random and this is what he came up with.

No. 13
Death   Six of Wands   Eight of Pentacles   Queen of Pentacles

Referring to the instructions above, the only Major Arcana card is the Death card which suggests that a major change is about to take place in Simon's way of life. There is one Wand card and two Pentacles so business, money and resources are important factors here. The one Court card in the group denotes a practical, reliable and materialistic woman.

The interpretation might read as follows: 'Simon is soon going to change his way of life in an important way. This change will come as a result of a successful ending of something which is already in progress (Death = change and Six of Wands = success). He will take a new job or otherwise improve his prospects at work (Eight of Pentacles) and a woman will figure in his life in some important way.'

This all seems very logical as Simon was not only running a small business with my son, Stuart, at the time of the reading, but the two lads were also on the way to finishing a degree course in computer and business studies. The cards indicated a success for Simon and either an expansion of the two lads' small business or a successful spell out at work. Simon had an important girlfriend at the time of the reading.

(Between this reading having been made and the book going to press, I can confirm the outcome of the situation: Simon got his degree, is living with his girlfriend, has taken a good job and still has time to do some business with my son!)

Examples to try for yourself

Example 1

| | No. 10 | | No. 6 |
| Ace of Swords | Wheel of Fortune | Six of Swords | The Lovers |

Here we find two Major Arcana cards and two Sword cards. The immediate impression is that this reading refers to something important, because the presence of more than one Major card in such a small spread suggests that the hand of fate is very strongly involved here. The Wheel of Fortune is a particularly 'fateful' card and the Swords are the most serious and 'heavy' of the four suits.

A brief clue to the interpretation
Here we have two Major Arcana cards which, linked together, suggest a change in relationships. The Wheel suggests change and The Lovers suggests choices which are concerned with our relationship to others. There are two Sword cards which suggest important decisions which must be taken by the Questioner. The Ace of Swords puts power in the hands of the Questioner. These decisions may be related to travel due to the presence of the Six of Swords, or moving on from one way of life to another. The Wheel suggests change while the Six of Swords denotes movement. The Lovers may indicate a new companion. Swords suggest serious matters while The Lovers suggest choices to be made.

Now go back and look at that list again and see what *you* can make of it for yourself. Use your imagination to fill the story out and make it entertaining.

Example 2

Two of Pentacles   Two of Cups   King of Pentacles   Eight of Pentacles

Groupings
Two Cup cards and two Twos. One Court card.

Interpretation
This reading screams 'relationships' to me. See what you can make of it.

Example 3

                        No. 4   No. 13
Nine of Swords   The Emperor   Death   Eight of Cups

The odd one out here is the Emperor. All the others talk about leaving something or someone behind.

Example 4

No. 10	No. 8	No. 0	
Wheel of Fortune	Strength	The Fool	Page of Cups

With three Major Arcana cards and one Minor Arcana, the reading is clearly in the hands of fate rather than the hands of the Questioner. The Page of Cups here assumes a greater importance than it otherwise might *because* it is the only Minor card in the spread.

Now try this method of reading the cards for yourself and your friends.

Chapter 9

A Back-to-Front Experiment

The theory of 'Super Tarot' is to work in a completely back-to-front manner by choosing the cards which will illustrate a particular story, rather than by looking at the cards which turn up in a reading and trying to interpret them. The point of this approach is to encourage you to think about the cards in logical groups which will describe the story which you want told. If this works the way I think it will, it should solve your 'stringing cards together' problems for once and for all.

The idea is to look at a situation and then *to pick the cards which describe it*. The choice of cards is, of course, totally yours. Whilst thinking about this chapter, I experimented on some of my Tarot reading friends by asking them to pick out a selection of cards which would indicate a move of house. The results were extraordinary; *everyone chose different cards*! When I asked them why they had chosen their particular cards, they all had equally sensible reasons for having done so. This made me go back and look at the cards more closely and as a result, I have modified some of my own feelings about several of them.

This chapter is illustrated with cards from *The Servants of the Light Tarot* by Dolores Ashcroft-Nowicki, painted by Jo Gill (Major Arcana) and Anthony Clark (Minor Arcana). In this deck the suits are named Weapons (Swords), Crescents (Cups), Staves (Wands) and Spheres (Pentacles). The Court cards have become Maker (King), Giver (Queen), User (Knight) and Keeper (Page).

Demonstration

Let us suppose that we are engaged upon a reading which is telling us that our Questioner is about to get a new job. There are plenty of cards which denote a new start — for instance, all the Aces as well as many, possibly

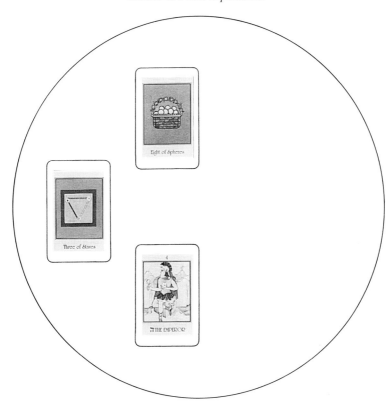

most, of the Major Arcana cards. However, for the purposes of this example I have chosen three cards which seem suitable:

1. The Eight of Pentacles is often seen as a 'new-job' card by Tarot Readers. It certainly suggests satisfying, creative work to be done.
2. The Three of Wands suggests a new project, probably in company with a group of other people.
3. The Emperor suggests an improvement in one's status and general situation in life, which could well involve a new job offering potential benefits.

Let us now look at these potential benefits or otherwise which might arise from this new job to see what they might be.

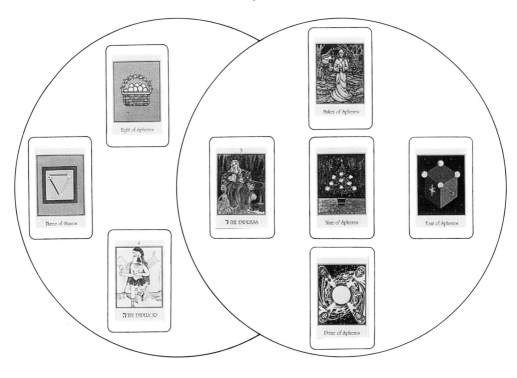

Overlay No. 1

The cards which I have selected for this overlay suggest that the Questioner will earn a lot of money from her new job. The Ace of Pentacles usually denotes a windfall, the Four implies security, the Nine and The Empress both relate to abundance and fertility, while the King would suggest an improvement in the Questioner's status and financial position. The King could also denote the Questioner's boss or perhaps her bank manager.

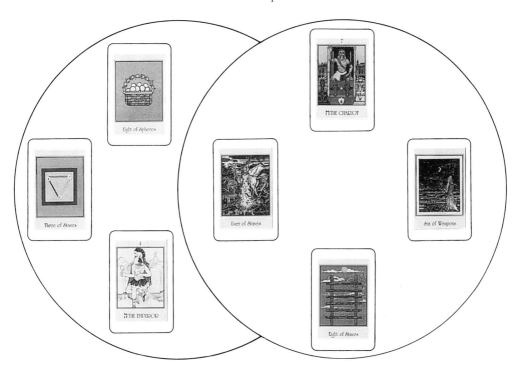

Overlay No. 2

This suggests that the new job will lead to opportunities for travel and a widening of horizons. The Six of Swords, The Chariot and the Eight of Wands are all cards which tend to denote travel (among other things), while the Knight of Wands is also associated with movement.

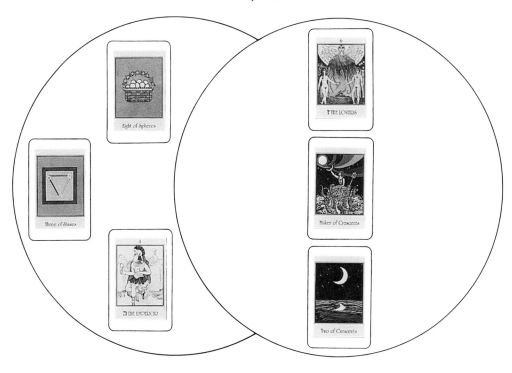

Overlay No. 3

This suggests that the job will lead to an improvement in the Questioner's social life. The Lovers card and the Two of Cups denote friendship, socializing and even romance, while the Knight of Cups could be a loving and friendly young man.

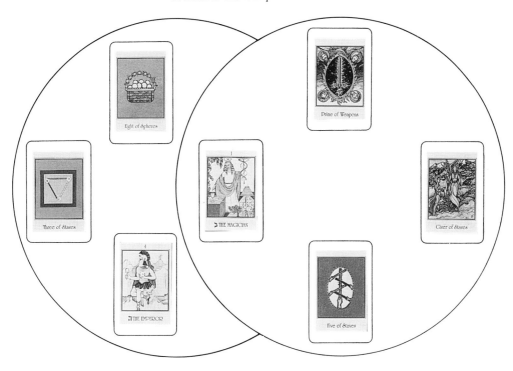

Overlay No. 4

This offers the Questioner an opportunity to improve her entrepreneurial skills. Self-employment, or at least self-determination, is probable too. The Magician denotes using skills and knowledge, good marketing techniques and self-determination, while the Ace of Swords puts power in the hands of the Questioner. The Five of Wands suggests a challenge, while the Queen of Wands is often associated with an enterprising and capable businesswoman.

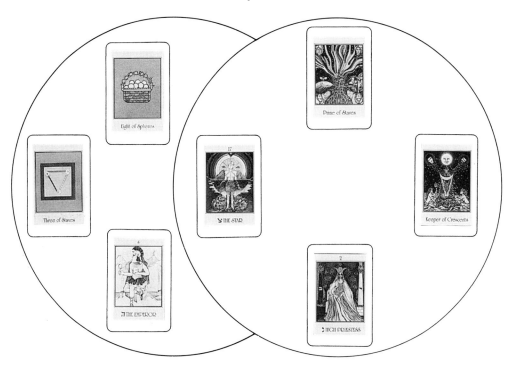

Overlay No. 5

This indicates that the job will offer training or education and an opportunity for the Questioner to better herself in the future. The Star denotes an expansion of knowledge and the ability to plan for the future, while the Ace of Wands suggests a new and rather creative outlook and also the birth of something new. The Priestess and the Page of Cups both have connections with training and education.

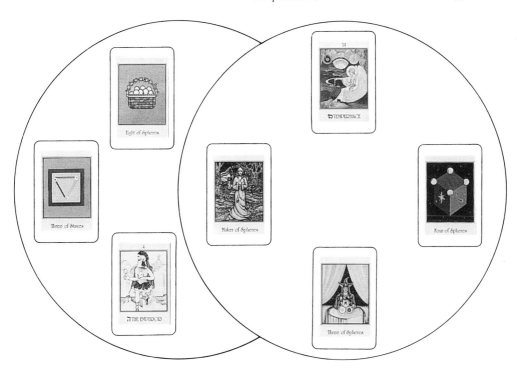

Overlay No. 6

This is a little more subtle as it means that the job will offer both peace and security. The Temperance card denotes peace and moderation while the Four of Pentacles implies financial security. The King of Pentacles would suggest an improvement in the Questioner's status and financial position while also representing her boss or even the financial department of her firm. The Three of Pentacles relates to work being completed according to some kind of specific plan or instruction.

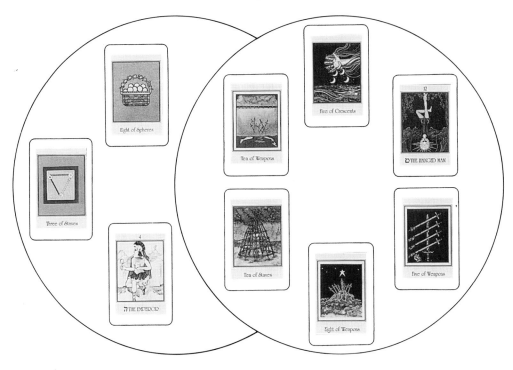

Overlay No. 7

The Five of Cups suggests that the job will be a disappointment, while the Ten of Wands shows a lot of hard work which may or may not be worth the effort. The Five of Swords denotes strife, while the Ten suggests either a stab in the back or a total dead-loss situation. The Eight of Swords shows that the Questioner will be either severely restricted in some way or even helpless, while The Hanged Man denotes sacrifice. If I saw something like this in the cards, I would tell my Questioner not to touch this job, because it could be hazardous as well as unpleasant.

Chapter 10

A Joint Venture

Now let us repeat the back-to-front experiment, but this time we will do it *together*. We will have a go at tackling the most popular question put by any Questioner to any Tarot Reader anywhere in the world. The Question is: 'How and when will I meet my future partner?' Of course the Questioner could be a man asking about the possibilities of finding a future wife but for the moment we will suppose that our Questioner is female. Answering the 'when' part of this question is very tricky, so I will leave this for now and tackle it in the chapter which deals with the timing of events.

Romantic meetings

There are any number of cards which could suggest an important man coming into a woman's life but the following three, taken here from Clive Barrett's *Norse Tarot*, are as good as any:

King of Cups

No. 6
The Lovers

Two of Cups

As you read through the 'overlay' stories it will be up to *you* to select cards which complete the back-to-front readings. It would be a good idea to pencil in the names of the cards you choose in the overlapping circle.

Overlay No. 1

Lea Stone works in a shop; her area manager is both pleasant and single. A friendship between them develops gradually over a period of about a year, then one day he comes into the shop when the other two staff are off sick. Perhaps the fact that this is the time of year for the annual stockcheck has something to do with the absence of the other two. Stocktaking is dirty and exhausting work, especially in such an old and dirty shop. The manager stays on to give the Questioner a hand, and it is while they are sitting on the floor behind the counter clutching a welcome mug of coffee, laughing at the state of their clothes and their dirty faces, that they begin to realize how much they like one another. He finds her very easy to talk to, and she is thinking how nice and kind he is and what a nice smile he has . . .

Overlay No. 2

She goes on holiday to Lanza-grotty with her best mate. The holiday is great fun and they meet plenty of young men of all nationalities but neither of them clicks with anyone. Now she is on her way home. During the inevitable delay at Aricife airport, she finds herself chatting to a slightly chubby young man from Croydon. Before the flight is called, they exchange addresses and agree to meet a week or so later. She is so pretty with her post-holiday tan and sun-streaked hair. His freckles almost join up over his nose and his reddish hair glows from the effects of the sun. They find many common interests and share a sense of the ridiculous ...

Overlay No. 3

She is a successful businesswoman. She manages her high-powered job as a buyer in a large electronics firm as well as her suburban home and her two attractive sons with great flair. It is now three years since her divorce and she would dearly love to meet someone special. Her friends are in the habit of inviting her to dinner parties where there is always a 'spare man' but these men always seem to have the air of the reject about them. The Questioner would rather remain alone than compromise. One day, one of her friends asks her to help out at a local fund-raising fete, telling her that she should bring the children along to help. Goodness knows, she is tired enough at the end of a hard week but, for the sake of the children and in order not to offend her friend, she agrees. The guy who is managing the event sends her friend and her children off to help set up the tombola while our Questioner is directed to help with putting up a marquee. She finds herself working alongside a tall, curly-haired chap who knows as little about tents as she does. They get into a terrible muddle but eventually get the awful thing put up. Her companion suggests a drink to cool off and while they are enjoying a much-needed lager, they begin to talk. He has been divorced for some years and has custody of his younger daughter ...

Now you not only get to choose the cards, you write the story as well!

Overlay No. 4

She crashes her trolley into his outside the local supermarket ...

Overlay No. 5

She goes to her friend's firm's disco ...

Overlay No. 6

He is a member of an archery club that her children belong to. One Saturday, they drag her along to see the championships ...

Overlay No. 7

She joins a teacher-training course and falls for the lecturer . . .

If nothing else this chapter should teach you the very valuable lesson that you must use your *imagination*. Soon we will have a go at some storylines the right way round (that is, cards first — story after) and you will see how valuable it is to be able to weave a story out of the cards in front of you. It will feel at first as if you are making the whole thing up: don't worry and don't stop; just follow your imagination because it will inevitably lead you to the right interpretation.

The mechanism which makes this work is terribly simple. It is just that as you relax and allow your mind to reach for a story to fit the cards, your spiritual guides will gather near and nudge your brain and tongue into giving the right answers. You are never alone when reading the Tarot.

A sad story

In this section I will tell you a sad tale and allow you to follow the plot through the cards which I have selected as an illustration. Let us assume that a Questioner is asking us about the future of his marriage which appears to be on the rocks. Once again, we will use no special spread, simply groups of cards which we will choose to tell the story.

The tension builds up

Nine of Swords	Worry, fear, sleepless nights.
Five of Pentacles	Loss, financial worry.
Five of Cups	Loss, sadness, regret, looking backwards but considering what is left with which to start a new life.

The crisis

Five of Swords	Quarrels, strife, conflict, anger, rage.
Death	Major change, transformation is imminent.
The Tower	Collapse of previous way of life.
Ten of Swords	Collapse of way of life, complete ending.
Three of Swords	Separation.

The practicalities

Two of Pentacles	Separation of assets.

Eight of Cups	Turning away from something, walking away.
Justice	Legal matters (also a fair outcome).
Judgement	End of a situation (this card also has legal connotations).
King of Swords	A lawyer.
Seven of Swords	Legal advice, also moving on and making a fresh start.

Negative or reversed cards

If you use negative or reversed cards in your readings, all the 'making a relationship' cards can be used to denote the ending of one. Therefore, the Two of Cups, Three of Cups and The Lovers in the reversed mode can be used for this, as can many other cards (see page 104).

Over to you

In the following exercises, I will suggest some situations and you must choose the cards to fit them. If it helps you to make a note of the reason for your choices you may do so. You can use a separate sheet of paper if you don't want to scribble all over your book.

Your selection of cards for a new home

Major Arcana cards   *Why chosen*

Minor Arcana cards   *Why chosen*

Major Arcana cards   *Why chosen*

The start of a romance

Major Arcana cards   *Why chosen*

Minor Arcana cards   *Why chosen*

A family quarrel

Major Arcana cards	*Why chosen*

Minor Arcana cards	*Why chosen*

Now try the following:

(a) A health warning.
(b) Overseas travel.
(c) A financial loss.
(d) A relationship which starts well, then peters out.
(e) Advising against a house-move.

Chapter 11

Games Which Will Stretch Your Imagination

Flowchart

The following example is intended to set you thinking. This kind of idea can be used to look at a specific opportunity and see what the possibilities are. This is one way in which you can ask questions and perhaps get some useful answers in an unusual and interesting manner.

The world is full of possibilities

Let us assume that our Questioner is a single man living in his own rented flat. He has a girlfriend whom he likes very much but is not yet seriously considering engagement or marriage. His parents, with whom he has a good relationship, live close by. He is a normal young man with a reasonable sense of adventure but up till now, has never seriously contemplated doing anything other than living and working in his own neighbourhood. At the time of the reading, he has been offered a two-year contract in Vancouver. He fancies the idea of the trip but wonders how he will get on so far away from home. He is also looking at his relationship with his girlfriend and trying to assess his (and her) feelings at being parted for such a length of time. As our Questioner is a bright young man who is looking forward to enjoying the twenty-first century we will, in his honour, drag the Tarot out of its fusty medieval home and put it onto a computer flowchart.

How to use the flowchart

Begin with the oval at the top of the page which makes the statement 'Work overseas'. Then look at the questions in the oblong question box: 'The job? The money? Location?' The cards are named in the diamond-shaped processing box and the answers are to be found in the

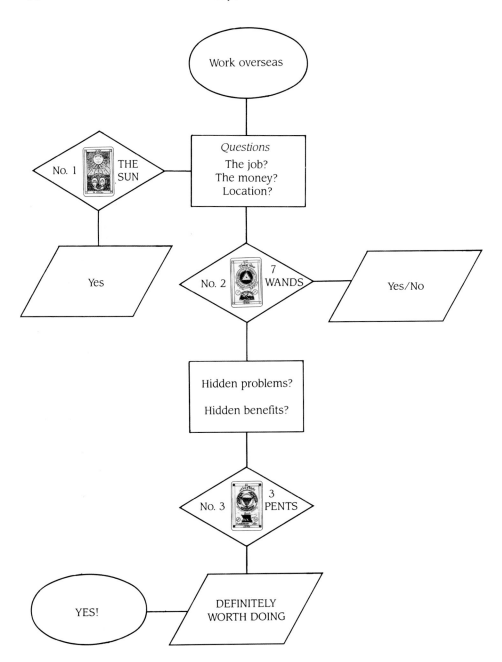

parallelogram-shaped answer boxes. Further questions can be found in the oblong question-boxes with the thinking processes in the diamond-shaped boxes and further answers in the parallelogram boxes. All clear? No? Well look at the diagram and go with the flow.

The question here is: 'Shall I take this job in Vancouver?' If the cards were in the mood to be kind to us, they would give a nice clear answer such as the one below:

The Sun This card suggests success on all levels, therefore the answer would be to take the job and not to worry too much about the details as they will soon be ironed out.

Only too often the cards give a confusing 'maybe' answer, in which case a bit more digging will be required.

The Seven of Wands This card suggests that there will be problems, possibly quite a few of them, but there is nothing to suggest that they cannot be overcome.

Now we ask if there are any hidden difficulties or benefits which will come to light after the man starts the job.

The   This card has two meanings: the first one
Three of   shows that the work will go well and the
Pentacles   results will be worthwhile to all concerned, while the second meaning sug-
gests that housing may be particularly
good in that part of the world, with the
possible implication that the girlfriend
may wish to join the Questioner living in
Vancouver.

If this were a genuine reading, three cards would hardly be enough to give
a worthwhile answer; something deeper, such as the Celtic Cross spread
would be much better.

A snakes and ladders game
with no snakes and no ladders

The following idea (shown here using the *Prediction* deck) makes a
pleasant break from all the hard work which you have been putting in and
it will help you and your friends to get to grips with assessing cards very
quickly. You will need one dice and as many counters as players. There are
two sets of rules for this game which are as follows:

1. The first player must roll the dice and move the counter forward
   according to the number shown. He must then assess the card upon
   which the counter lands. If he considers this to be a very good card,
   he should move his counter forward two places. If he considers it to
   be fairly good, then he can move forward one place. If the card appears
   to be really bad, he should move backwards two places. If he considers
   it to be only slightly bad, he should move backwards one place.
2. The second instruction is simple — cheat!

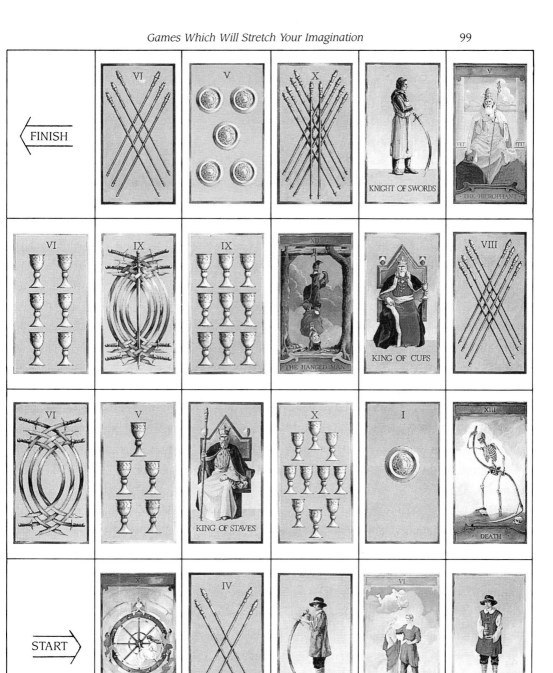

Chapter 12

A Trivial Pursuit

The Tarot cards have often been compared to a journey through life. Indeed, many people teach the Major Arcana in the form of a journey starting with The Fool who is like a new-born baby who knows nothing about the journey ahead of him, and ending with The World which represents the completion of our journey here on earth. However, in this section of the book, we will take the simple idea of running down a country lane and see what kind of journey the cards offer us.

The idea is simply to follow the little cartoon man's trivial pursuit which is marked by arrows and look at each card which he meets along the way. I have suggested an interpretation for the course of the first of these journeys, both of which are illustrated with cards from Courtney Davis's *Celtic Tarot*.

The journey

The Significator, or card which represents the traveller, is the King of Wands. This is appropriate because the Wands are adventurous and enthusiastic and much given to travelling.

The first cards which he meets on the way are the Three of Pentacles together with the King of Swords. This shows that he could end his journey here because the Three of Pentacles is offering him the chance of a stable home or job at this point, but also a lot of work to be done. The King can advise him on these matters but can also guide him on his way if he chooses to travel on.

Now the road forks and, for the moment, our traveller takes the right-hand fork. The first two cards on this road are rather good. The Knight of Cups travels with him for a while, offering him friendship and fun along the way while the Temperance card suggests that the scenery is beautiful and the journey peaceful. However this road peters out and the Two of Swords shows that this way leads to nothing but stalemate. He must retrace his steps and try the other fork.

The left-hand fork soon brings him to the Six of Swords which is clearly a card of travel and therefore pointing him in the right direction. With this card is the Five of Wands which denotes a challenge which can be entered into with enjoyment and with every chance of success to follow. After this he meets the Six of Pentacles which means that he will have to find money for a hotel for the night. There are travelling mendicants outside the hotel and he proffers a coin or two to help them out. They wish him good luck.

After a good night's sleep, he decides to investigate a sideroad before returning to the main road. This turns out to be a mistake as he trips over a low wall and nearly falls into a water-logged quarry. This reminds him that life is not always easy, then he pulls himself back onto the main road and meets yet another companion.

This time the companion is a practical woman as signified by the Queen of Pentacles. The Six of Cups denotes that she has two children with her who remind him of the family he will be seeing again at the end of his journey.

Finally he arrives at the end of the journey. The Justice card shows that the journey was worth it. He has set things right in his life and his experiences have brought balance and understanding to his mind. He will find a sense of equilibrium and a reasonable way of life now that his travels are over.

Now over to you again

The second pathway is for you to play with. Give it to your friends in turn and see what each one makes of it. See how many stories you can get out of it. This may only be a bit of harmless fun, but it will stretch your knowledge of the cards and your ability to fit them together.

Chapter 13

Some Helpful Hints

Reading for yourself or for others

As a change from all the games and exercises and a reward for all your hard work, I'll let you take a rest now while I answer some commonly-asked questions for you. Many people want to know whether they can read the cards for themselves or whether it would be unlucky to do so. The answer is that you *can* read the cards for yourself and that it is not at all unlucky to do so. I think that the notion of self-reading being unlucky was put forward as a deterrent because reading for oneself is never very successful and if that is *all* you want to use the cards for, you will not get much out of them. Their purpose is to allow you to tune into other people and to do something to help sort out *their* lives, rather than concentrate on your own. It is difficult to take an objective view of the cards when reading for yourself because you are bound to try to fit them to what you know of your life and circumstances. It is also very hard to create a psychic link to yourself. Many beginners are tempted to read spread after spread for themselves which results in the cards losing all meaning thus putting them off reading the cards at all. Self-awareness and the ability to look into your own future are entirely reasonable objectives but Tarot is not a good vehicle for this. I suggest that you also take a look into some other form of divination, such as astrology or numerology for self-analysis as this will not only be interesting but will ultimately help your Tarot studies.

There is one method of self-reading which might be worth experimenting with and that is to lay out the cards and analyse them as objectively as you can. Write your findings down, date the piece of paper and put it away for a few weeks, then take it out again and check the accuracy of your reading. The same method can be tried out on family and close friends.

The Significator

A card can be chosen to signify a person or situation. The choice of card is entirely personal.

Reversed cards

It is unfashionable to use reversed cards these days, however they can come in handy at times. A reversed Court card suggests that the person is not on the side of the Questioner while any reversed card can work against itself. For instance, the three of cups suggests a relationship which should not or will not end in marriage while the Eight of Wands suggests a trying journey and jealous companions.

Specific advice for aspiring psychics

Any form of study which has a psychic content will help develop your Tarot reading skills. Your choice of psychic study will depend upon your own particular taste. For example, the people at your local Spiritualist Church will help you to train as a medium while a dowser or diviner will show you how to find things, to diagnose illness and to look for ley lines. Psychometry is the art of holding an object and feeling or seeing something of its past history and this is often taught as a means of enhancing receptivity by Spiritualist development circles. Any kind of class or workshop which covers any of these subjects will help. The main thing is to be able to open your chakras (the psychic centres of the body) and, far more importantly, to be able *to close them down again afterwards*. There are many ways of visualizing these chakras but the following list (which was given to me by an excellent psychic called Barbara Ellen) is as good as any.

1. The base chakra which you can visualize as a red poppy.
2. The spleen chakra which you can visualize as an orange marigold.
3. The solar plexus chakra which you can visualize as a yellow daisy.
4. The heart chakra which you can visualize as two green doors.
5. The throat chakra which you can visualize as a turquoise light.
6. The forehead chakra (also called the third eye) which you can visualize as a deep blue eye.
7. The crown chakra which you can visualize as an amethyst-coloured lily.

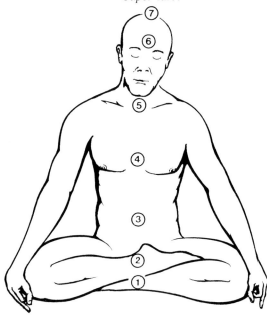

The colours of the chakras are the same as the colours of the rainbow.

If you wish to open the chakras in preparation for any kind of psychic or intuitive work, visualize a white light being beamed down and in from the Universe to the top of your head. As it reaches your head, mentally open the crown chakra, then bring the light down to the forehead chakra and open that. The light will then need to be brought down to each of the remaining chakras, halted for a moment while you open them, and then taken down through the soles of your feet.

You will need to make a conscious effort to open these chakras while you are developing your intuitive skills but as soon as you know that 'things' are happening, you will only rarely need to make the effort: they will open quickly enough each time you start to work. Closing these chakras is much more important and *has* to be done every time you finish any kind of psychic work or experiment. Simply turn off the light up as far as the lowest chakra and close that down; then rise upwards through the remaining chakras, closing them down one at a time and turning off the light, finally sending it back out to the Universe. You will find that you can do this very quickly with practise. After the close-down, I suggest that you strengthen your aura by imagining yourself getting into a sleeping-bag and doing it up all the way round and then over your head so that you are totally enclosed. If you don't bother with this 'closing down ceremony' you may be plagued by bad dreams, psychic disturbances or a feeling of depression due to 'picking up' other peoples' problems, worries and negative thoughts. I suggest that even if you have only been listening to a friend pouring her heart out on the phone that you use the sleeping-bag technique afterwards to remove her negativity from your aura.

Responsibility

If the cards suggest that the present is all right but that there will be problems in the future, be very positive and suggest ways in which the Questioner can best handle things. Be reasonably honest, but don't leave your Questioner feeling hopeless. A health warning may save someone's life but undue stress and worry can kill, so be careful and think what you are doing. If your Questioner is neurotic and negative by nature, it may be better to avoid the worst of the bad news as this can prey on his or her mind and even turn into a self-fulfilling prophecy. If you are unsure of what you are seeing in the cards, or of your ability to read them correctly, then err on the side of optimism. You need to strike a balance between your own credibility as a reader and causing unnecessary suffering. Remember that you will inevitably influence your clients in the decisions they take, even if your role is only to clarify their own minds. Remember also to trust your gut feelings and your spiritual guides. The Questioner also bears a certain responsibility, in that he or she has elected to have a reading and therefore should be prepared to hear whatever is said, whether it be good or bad news. Unfortunately very few Questioners realize this. I also take the view that if I am being shown that something unpleasant is about to befall my Questioner, it is essential for me to pass this on as a warning.

Prejudices

I briefly mentioned the subject of prejudice in the Court card section and I offer no apology for returning to it now. In the Court card section I demonstrated that the client's own point of view would be shown on the cards. If you remember, I used the scenario of a woman who wanted her lover to leave his wife and who considered the wife to be a hard-hearted bitch for hanging on to him. We also showed that the wife's reading of the situation could just as easily be that the mistress was the bitch. Whilst we must take the client's point of view into consideration, we have to leave our own outside the door and look at each client as no more than a human being who wants help and advice at that particular moment. If you become a professional Reader you will find yourself dealing with people from every part of the world and every possible culture and walk of life. Some of these people will be on your own personal wavelength, many of them will not, but each client's money is as good as the next and each needs a sensible and unbiased reading.

Chapter 14

Tarot Reading as a Profession

Practical advice

Some of you reading this book may be contemplating the possibility of becoming a professional Tarot Reader. This may be because you fancy the idea, or because you have been reading cards for your friends for a long time and are now being asked by strangers if you would read for them. You may decide to take up a career as a Reader because you are short of money and on the lookout for some additional form of income, or there may be any one of a number of other reasons. The first point I would like to make here is that it is perfectly alright to offer Tarot readings in exchange for money — you won't be punished by some kind of unseen force for doing so. However, for the sake of both your clients and yourself, you must know what you are doing, so therefore do make sure that you are as confident as possible in your reading skills and that you can cope with the people and the problems with which you will be faced. It might be helpful to take a course in counselling techniques, even if you don't actually use these during your readings, and it is always worth visiting a few other Readers to see how they go about things.

Other necessary skills

If you are only going to give a few readings here and there for pin money, you will not need to worry about the following advice, but if you are considering making Tarot reading into a career, you will need to take it on board.

Firstly, you will need somewhere to give your readings. Your own home is the cheapest place and, if possible, you can set a room aside for the purpose and decorate it in any style which you deem to be appropriate. If you cannot spare a room, at least make sure that the area which you do use is tidy, warm and pleasant to look at. To be honest, I have found that people are usually so keen to have their readings that they will put up with almost anything, and when my office-cum-consulting room has been out of action for some reason, my clients have happily had their readings in the kitchen, the garden, the bedroom or the hallway. Noise and interruptions are a far greater problem than the actual location of the reading, so try to keep the area as quiet and peaceful as possible with pets and children kept out of the way. You will also need somewhere for clients to wait, especially if two people come together. A couple of chairs in the hall may be suitable for this but don't forget to provide a magazine for the client to look at while waiting.

You will need some basic business equipment. Whether you advertise your services or not, you will need a telephone and perhaps an answering machine. The answering machine is not only useful for those occasions when you are out, but can be switched on while you are with a client in order to prevent interruptions. If you become busy in your new career, you will find it a great relief to be able to switch the machine on when you don't want to be bothered by calls because the public don't stop to think about the time or the day before lifting up the phone. A desk diary is also a must, as are printed business cards and/or information sheets which can be handed on by your clients to their friends.

If you don't want to work alone from home, you may take space at psychic fairs and festivals. In this case, you will need decorations for your stand and information as to who you are, what you do and how much you charge. One good thing about working at these festivals is that you meet other Readers and can exchange ideas and information.

If you become fully professional, you will have to use a sensible system of book-keeping and to keep receipts for all expenses. Don't forget that as a small business-person you will be allowed certain expenditures against income tax. These allowances vary from one country to another but there will be professional people who can advise you on them. You will also need a separate bank account in order to keep your working income separate from your household income. It is quite a good idea to talk to other small business-people and see how they manage. (I remember that my own excellent book-keeping and taxation advice came from a lady who ran a beauty parlour for dogs!) Make sure that you inform the relevant authorities of what you are doing and use an accountant or other qualified professional person to audit your books once a year.

You may fancy giving readings by phone or by post, in which case you may need to buy a typewriter or word-processor. One thing which you will almost inevitably need is a tape-recorder. Most professional Readers make a tape recording for the client to take away with them. A good tape-recorder will pick up your voice even from a slight distance and tapes can be bought fairly cheaply in bulk.

How to avoid picking up bad vibes

Unlike psychotherapy, medicine, chiropody, hairdressing or any other personal service, Tarot Readers have to work with their chakras open — whether they realize this or not. This is akin to going out into cold weather without a coat on. There is not much you can do about it, but your preparation and blessing of the cards when you first obtained them will probably afford you all the protection you need. You can always ask your spiritual guides for extra protection if needs be, simply by sending out a mental request to them, even in the middle of a reading.

Most clients are perfectly well-meaning but the odd one may leave you feeling uncomfortable in some undefinable way after a reading. If this happens, close your chakras, strengthen your aura and ask for cleansing and protection. A good shower and hairwash will get rid of any unpleasant vibes for good. You can always re-prepare your pack of cards again as if they were brand new. In the extremely unlikely event of your premises being invaded by something strange and unseen which may have been 'dumped' by a client, ask your guides to clean and protect the place and then mentally fill it from the ground upwards with imaginary clean, clear water. If you are ever worried by any of this, you can also consult a good spiritual medium for advice. It is unlikely that you will ever have to go to any of these lengths but at least you now know how to deal with these problems if they should arise.

Further dangers for the professional

There are other forms of danger for professional readers which are only too obvious when you begin to think about them. First of all, if you are going to have strangers coming and out of your home, you are in danger of being robbed, raped, hurt or even murdered. I have never actually heard of any professional being hurt, raped or murdered, but theft is all too common. I have lost a camera, ornaments and other bits and pieces to light-fingered clients. One of your clients might be a burglar who cannot resist coming back while you are out and helping himself to your property; alternatively a perfectly innocent client may gossip to someone else who is a burglar.

The only suggestion which I can make is that you think about these unpleasant possibilities and protect yourself against them before you start. The chances of anything going wrong are very small, if for no other reason than the fact that spirit tends to protect its own. However, it is as well to make sure that your home is secure when you are out and that the contents of your home are fully insured. Don't leave clients alone with your valuables and don't let them wander all over the house. Many clients have a sudden urge to use the bathroom when visiting a consultant, possibly due to nerves. Make sure that your bedroom doors are shut so that the client doesn't start looking around and so that you can hear if they open any door unnecessarily. If there is a public lavatory near you, it might be as well to send them there. I know this sounds harsh, but you will have to work out whether you need to adopt these precautions or not based on where you work.

If you are a woman, I suggest that you only see male clients when other members of your family are around. Otherwise restrict yourself only to men that you know and trust or to women or couples. Fortunately the majority of clients are usually female. If anybody of either sex begins to talk to you in a way which makes you feel uneasy, then get rid of them fast and don't let them come to you again. To be honest, the chances of anything nasty happening are extremely remote, but as with the problems of bad vibes and psychic attack, it is as well to be aware of the dangers.

Failed readings

If you are an amateur and you experience the strange phenomenon of giving a reading where you just can't get anything right, this may put you off doing any more. Don't let it! There are many reasons for failed readings. If you are a professional and you go through a bad patch, then this can shake your confidence and even make you give up the job for good. One failure is not worth worrying about, but a series of them will require some action on your part.

In the case of a professional Reader having an isolated failure the only thing to do is to send the client away without accepting any fee. Tell him or her that it is just one of those things which happens from time to time and that he or she should come back to you in a couple of months time when whatever was blocking the reading may have gone and go to someone else for a reading in the meantime. You may have a friend or a colleague whom you can recommend.

Readings can go wrong for many reasons. The following list shows some possibilities:

1. You may be ill or otherwise having an 'off' day, or you may have eaten or drunk too much. An over-full stomach blocks the workings of some of the chakras while too much 'booze' can block everything. Oddly enough, one drink can be useful as a relaxant but more than one will mess everything up!
2. Clients may have some kind of blockage around them, which neither

you nor they can see or understand. This may be caused by *their* spirit guides who don't think that they should have a reading at this particular time.

3. Clients' spirit guides may want them to have a reading but *not with you*! This is very hard on your ego, but it is possible that a client's guides want him/her to be in contact with and to trust another consultant. I remember one occasion when I couldn't get anywhere with a client however much I tried and, having confidence in my skills, I immediately realized that her guides must be blocking me for a reason. After this non-event reading, we chatted for a while and it turned out that the lady had seen another Reader some distance away and had been asked by her to join a psychic development circle. I myself was aware that this client was very psychic and that she should be doing something to develop her talents. It seemed as if spirit wanted her to have complete faith and trust in this other Reader, so that she would trust her as a teacher.

4. There are people for whom you will never be able to read, either because you are completely out of sympathy with that type of person, or because you dislike each other on sight. We have discussed personal prejudices earlier in the book but, with the best will in the world, you cannot *always* set these aside.

5. Another problem is that people who seek readings may be in a distressed state of mind which may make them angry or hostile. They may take out their anger on you and while you may understand this and make allowances for it, you don't have to put up with it. One of the joys of being self-employed is that you don't have to take any 'stick' from anyone and you are perfectly entitled to show any unwelcome client the door.

6. Your client may be crazy. You are not a psychiatrist and you don't have to deal with this. Another possibility is that a client may be so stupid that he or she cannot understand the reading even if it does work.

7. If you are weighed down by problems in your own life you will find it hard to tune in to someone else's. You may even feel resentful of the demands which the Questioner makes on you. The only answer is to leave Tarot reading for a while and do something completely different. Take a holiday, if you can afford to, and come back to work when you are feeling better or happier. This happens to us all from time to time. We are not machines; psychic work takes a great deal of effort and this may be your guides' way of making you switch off and take a break.

Referrals

Be prepared to suggest that your client visit his or her doctor or dentist, insurance broker or bank manager. You may wish to refer a client on to a counsellor or psychotherapist, a woman's group, drug centre or any other help agency or self-help group. It may be useful to keep a list of such groups handy, but if not, suggest that clients start by asking their own doctors who usually know where to refer people for more help.

Finally

Keep your readings to a fairly rigid timescale of no more than an hour. One way of doing this is to book all your clients in on the same day so that each one is aware of the arrival of the next one. This prevents clients taking advantage of your good nature and staying too long. It is also easier to open your chakras, do a day's work and then close them again for good rather than open them for an hour or so here and there. If clients try to phone back and discuss their readings in great detail after the event, tell them that you cannot remember the details. The chances are that this will be the plain unvarnished truth, because as you close your chakras and get on with your own life once more, a good deal of the content of the day's readings will be erased from your mind. Many clients will ask you questions when they enquire about readings. Most of these questions are quite reasonable ones such as how much you charge and how long a reading is likely to take. Some people, also quite reasonably, will ask how far into the future you can see. However, there are some people who will begin to discuss their problems and try to push you into giving what amounts to a free reading there and then. Remember, if you are in business, you will need to be businesslike. This is your job and nobody, not even your friends, should feel that they are entitled to receive 'freebies'. If you decide voluntarily to give a reading to a friend then by all means do so, but you must protect yourself from drainers and vampires.

What to charge

The answer to this is simple. Find out what other Readers in your neighbourhood charge and charge the same. You may wish to charge a bit less than the average while you are building up your clientele, but once you have got going, you can raise your prices. I have always used my own patent 'hairdresser' scale, which means that I charge roughly the amount a woman (most clients are women) is prepared to spend on a good hair-do.

Chapter 15

Laying Out the Cards

Spreads

From now on we will be looking not only at the cards themselves, but at the spreads and layouts which amplify their meanings. We will also look at the timing of events and other specialized forms of information as well as reviewing the cards in various different ways.

The spreads in this chapter are illustrated using Clive Barrett's *Norse Tarot.*

A simple layout

This spread is inspired by watching an acquaintance of mine reading playing-cards. She uses no specific spread but simply fifteen cards taken at random from the whole pack and then spread out on the table. The point of this kind of reading is to see which cards are next to one another and how they modify each other. This adds a little depth to the reading.

The example here is a general reading for no-one in particular and for no specific purpose. Let us assume for the moment that *you* are the Questioner and that this is *your* reading. We will approach this in the same way that we would a school cookery, maths or biology project, where we have to consider the method before doing the job itself.

Random reading no. 1: Thinking phase

There are fifteen cards here and they fall into the following categories:

(a) Three Major Arcana cards
(b) Three Court cards
(c) Two Aces
(d) Five Wand cards
(e) Three Pentacle cards

Random reading no. 1

(f)   Three Cup cards
(g)   One Sword card.

Three Major Arcana cards in a spread of fifteen is slightly fewer than one would expect and this suggests that the future is in your *own* hands rather than the hands of fate. Three Court cards in a spread like this is about average, which suggests that other people will have a normal effect on your immediate future. Two Aces are more than one might expect, so fresh starts of one kind or another are likely. Three Pentacle and three Cup cards are about average, but the number of Wand cards is high and there is only one Sword card. The feeling surrounding this reading therefore is of enthusiasm for the future, high ideals and a very busy period ahead. There seems to be one rather important worry, but this is not a time of major loss or crisis. In short, normal, everyday life is indicated.

The reading

The World card indicates that a phase of your life is coming to a natural conclusion, but The Devil close by shows that you are finding it difficult to let go of something. The Five of Wands with the Ace of Pentacles close by denote challenges ahead resulting in financial benefit. The Queen of Wands, on the other side of the Ace, shows that a clever businesslike woman will be instrumental in helping you in your endeavours. Above The World card, the Two of Cups suggests important meetings with friendly people, while the Two of Wands further down suggests that these will be connected with work or property rather than love. The presence of two Twos in this reading suggests an atmosphere of ço-operation. At the top of the spread, the Ten of Swords shows that something is going to turn out badly and the Four of Cups next to it endorses this, but also tells us that this is not a total loss. The Ten of Pentacles reaffirms that money is on the way and that this may be the start of a much better financial future. It also suggests laying the foundations for something long-lasting. The Eight of Wands alongside the Ten and below the Four of Cups denotes travel, while the Ace of Wands below suggests that this is connected with a creative project. A kindly, friendly man, as suggested by the King of Cups, will be involved in this enterprise. Below the King, the Page of Pentacles shows that small improvements in your finances are connected with this man. The Hanged Man at the bottom of the spread denotes that none of these events will happen quickly and that they will involve some form of sacrifice or 'letting go' in order to clear the way for the success which is to come.

Précis

To put all this in a nutshell: you will be busy, you will receive help, and your finances are on the up and up, but this will involve much concentration on work, possibly to the detriment of social life, relationships and some familiar aspect of your past. None of this seems to be serious but you will need courage and enterprise in order to take advantage of the opportunities for travel and expansion which seem to be on the way.

Random reading no. 2: A joint effort

Now let us do one together. Using the same kind of spread, this time I will do the thinking and you will do the interpreting.

(a) Three Major Arcana cards
(b) No Court cards
(c) One Ace
(d) Three Wand cards
(e) Three Cup cards
(f) Three Pentacle cards
(g) Three Sword cards.

Three Major cards in a spread this size is slightly fewer than can be expected, which signifies that this reading concerns the Questioner's *own* decisions and choices. This is confirmed by the absence of Court cards. The exact balance between the suits suggests that the Questioner is

---

Your Interpretation

Random reading no. 2

pondering over decisions which will affect every aspect of his life, while the single Ace shows that he is keen to make some kind of fresh start. The fact that this is the Ace of *Swords* further confirms that the Questioner wants to make his own decisions and to run his own life.

Now, over to you to see what you can make of the spread — you can use the box on page 117. I can't resist pointing out that The Moon, close by the revresed Three of Cups, could refer to a decision against a marriage.

Random reading no. 3: Another joint venture

This time we will do things the other way round. I will interpret the reading but you will do the thinking and planning.

The four Major cards suggest travel, expansion of horizons, a major turning-point and sunshine. There is also an indication that children or young people will soon become a part of the Questioner's life. The King of Wands next to The Chariot denotes travel and communications, while the Page of Wands tells us that the Questioner will soon have to learn something new (the King could be a teacher). The Ten and the Ace of Pentacles show that the Questioner's finances are tied up with the King figure while the Seven of Wands shows that problems will be reasonably easy to solve. The Queen of Wands at the top of the spread is also near the Page but hedged in on two sides by the difficult cards, the Ten of Swords and the Five of Pentacles. This juxtaposition suggests that a new venture will be disappointing, costly or hard to get off the ground. The Sun is bracketed by three Wand cards which show stability (the Nine), partnerships (the Two), and an ability to separate out and handle forthcoming problems (the Seven). The World and The Wheel of Fortune both suggest a phase coming to an end and the start of something new, while the Seven of Swords, stuck out on its own, means moving onwards but with the aid of legal or business advice.

Précis

This is an awkward reading to précis but my feeling is that the Questioner is embarking upon business negotiations which may include the rent of new property (Two of Wands) in association with foreigners, import and export, or travel. This seems fairly well-starred although one person may let him down (the Queen of Wands is not well placed in this reading). It may not be the best decision he has ever taken but there is a feeling of fate or inevitability about it (World, Wheel, Sun and Ace of Pentacles) and it also appears that things will work out well from the point of view of money (Ten and Ace of Pentacles).

Random reading no. 3

Now Go Back and Plan Your Reading Here

Random reading no. 4: Over to you

Now see what you can do with this one.

Planning The Reading

Random reading no. 4

Interpreting The Reading

Précis of The Interpretation

Naturally, no experienced Tarot Reader would approach a reading in such a highly-structured manner — Tarot reading is an intuitive skill while a school project is not. However, some amount of planning or observation should go on in your head before you plunge in. It is a case of engage brain before opening mouth. If you cannot remember the specific meaning of each card, go by the suit and type of card plus anything you pick up from the picture on it. This will help you to develop an instinctive approach rather than a purely logical one.

Chapter 16

The Simplest Form of Reading

Radio-Style Readings

Ever since my first book came out in 1985, I have been giving readings to phone-in listeners over the radio. This began as an occasional feature for my local radio station, and later developed into a regular programme on London Talkback Radio (LBC). The method I use is to ask listeners to take a pack of playing-cards (or Tarot cards if they have them), shuffle them and pick out six. The listener calls out each card to me one at a time, and I quickly translate this into a reading. In order to get any kind of meaningful reading, I have to use clairvoyance, intuition and the ability to translate playing-cards into their Tarot equivalent at high speed. This conversion is necessary because very few listeners have Tarot cards to hand, while practically everybody can lay their hands on a deck of playing-cards. Obviously, this kind of reading isn't easy to do, but after more than five years' constant practice, I have become very quick and accurate.

Sometimes I interpret each card singly, while on other occasions I will ask the listener to give me two together so that I can combine them. At the end of the reading, I usually précis my findings into a 'story', stringing the ideas together at great speed in order to achieve this. There is no time to make notes and the only thing I write down is the name of the listener.

Perhaps now you would like to have a go at this and see if you can speed up your feelings about a few cards in order to make a quick assessment of what is going on. Remember it is the energy behind each group of cards that we are searching for rather than specific meanings for each one. I will not add complications to your endeavours by substituting playing-cards for Tarot cards. Incidentally, when the occasional listener actually gives me Tarot cards to interpret, I find these *more* difficult to interpret than the Tarot-related playing-cards! There are a number of practical reasons for this. The first is that playing-cards are the equivalent of the Minor Arcana (with the exception of The Joker which is like The Fool) and it is actually *easier* to use Minor Arcana cards on their own for fast 'fortune-telling' of this kind, because the Major Arcana cards are too complicated to be interpreted at such speed. The second problem is that many people buy or are given a pack which only contains Major Arcana cards and it is exceedingly difficult to obtain a story from these alone. The third problem is that there are many hundreds of Tarot packs on the market, many of them of European origin, which means that I sometimes find myself struggling to understand a disembodied voice giving me names of cards which are unfamiliar to both of us in strangulated French, German, Spanish or Italian. Finally, by no means all the cards which are sold for divination purposes are actually Tarot! There are plenty of cards on the market which are totally unfamiliar to everyone except the person who invented them. Imagine trying to interpret a set of abstract shapes, or a series of bears, dogs, trees and mountains!

Well, those are *my* problems, now here come yours! As usual, I shall demonstrate the method first and then slowly begin to involve you in the sample readings. We are at a tremendous disadvantage because we know nothing about the people who are choosing these cards except their gender. Remember, we are going against all the rules of Tarot by reading these cards one-by-one instead of grouping them together. There is no time for considered thinking here, no weighing up of ratios, no time for counting or arranging the cards into groups. Let us plunge in and get on with it. The spreads are illustrated here with cards from *The Servants of the Light Tarot* — again, the traditional names are given in the text.

Our first 'caller' is female.

Prince of Crescents   User of Weapons   Prince of Staves   Eight of Spheres   Keeper of Weapons   Five of Staves

Card No. 1   The Ace of Cups. This card may represent a gift, a new lover, an impending marriage and/or the start of a joyous and happy time for you.

Card No. 2   The Knight of Swords. A young man is rushing into your life. He is active and energetic and should also be highly intelligent. The fact that he could also be aggressive is best kept to yourself for the time being.

Card No. 3	The Ace of Wands. This card signifies a new and very creative phase for you. The Ace of Wands can also denote the birth of a baby.
Card No. 4	The Eight of Pentacles. This card suggests a new job or promotion within your present job.
Card No. 5	The Page of Swords. A young man enters your life, he is energetic and intelligent. Alternatively, someone who is spying on your behalf.
Card No. 6	The Five of Wands. This suggests a challenge. A welcome new phase in your life which will keep you busy but also bring fun and happiness.

Well, in the case of a reading like this, it doesn't take a super-brain to work out that our listener is about to meet the love of her life, marry him and start a family. The 'work' card (Eight of Wands) is a bit off-putting here as it doesn't appear to fit in with the theme of the reading, but it could indicate that she will meet her guy at work or that she will work with him after they meet. The fact that the reading contains both the Page and the Knight of Swords to my mind simply emphasizes the tremendous importance that meeting this guy will have for the listener. Please go back and look at these cards again for yourself and see what *you* make of them. They may mean something quite different to you.

It is not easy for most Tarot Readers to give accurate readings over the radio or even over the phone, but if you do master this technique, it can be very useful. However, for the purposes of this book, you don't have to do any of these readings at a distance; you can try the technique out on your friends at home.

Joint ventures

Now let us work on a couple of these 'radio-style' readings together. In the first one, I shall outline the meanings of the cards and leave you to string them into a story, while in the second, I shall write the story and you will do the thinking. Then you *must* go back over them again and work out your own interpretations and stories for both of these readings because everyone reads the cards differently, and your ideas are more important to your Tarot reading development than mine.

Example 1

Let us assume for the purposes of this imaginary reading that our 'caller' is male.

1. The Five of Swords.
2. The Six of Cups.
3. The Sun.
4. The Ace of Swords.
5. The King of Wands.
6. The Emperor.

Reading the cards from left to right, I feel that this Questioner is about to find himself involved in a dispute. The dispute will have come from some past situation, even from as far back as his youth or childhood. The outcome seems to be beneficial but it will require a new way of looking at things and also a good deal of courage. His lines of communication will be clearer as a result of this dispute because those around him will know what it is that he wants and will negotiate reasonable terms with him. He will grow in status as a result of solving this problem.

Now Go Back and Work Out the Planning For This One

Example 2

Here are the six cards. The following imaginary caller is female:

1. *The Fool* A completely new beginning which could lead anywhere.
2. *Strength* Recovery after illness or a strong position within a situation. Tact and diplomacy will be needed.
3. *The Hermit* Retreat, reflection, patience and prudence. A wise advisor and spiritual enlightenment.
4. *Three of Pentacles* A move of house or work to be done on a house. Alternatively, a job of work to be done.
5. *Knight of Pentacles* A steady and steadfast youngish man. Something to do with money, resources and worthwhile occupations.
6. *Queen of Pentacles* Similar to the Knight but a female figure.

Now Go Back and Interpret The Reading

Example 3

The next one is all yours but it is slightly complicated by the fact that when I chose the cards, one of them turned out to be reversed. I shall leave this card just as it is and let you work out whether it has any significance or not. This time, you can choose the sex of your caller.

1. Six of Wands (reversed)
2. King of Pentacles
3. Ten of Pentacles
4. Five of Cups
5. Five of Swords
6. Queen of Cups

This One is All Yours To Plan and Then Interpret

Chapter 17

Timing By the Cards

There are various methods of timing events by Tarot cards, but none of them is foolproof. The problem is that Tarot is not 'scientific' in the way that astrology is. In astrology, the planets move at specific speeds and in particular directions and one planet is either aspecting another or it is not. Tarot is an intuitive and somewhat mediumistic skill, which means that any reading may be achieved as a result of what we can produce from our own psyche, aided or otherwise by our own spiritual guides and/or those of our Questioner. Timing devices depend upon the personal preference of each Tarot Reader, how he or she chooses to work and what he or she believes to be the truth. If you believe your readings to be spiritually guided or inspired, then you will have difficulty in timing events because the spirit world doesn't seem to measure time in the sense that we understand it. If you are practical rather than spiritual you will still experience problems because every Tarot reading is powered and driven by *emotion* and therefore the cards will inevitably be influenced by any event which produces strong feelings. Worse still, the event which caused these feelings may be in the past or the future and the poor Tarot Reader has no way of knowing which it may be.

One very frustrating experience is when a reading is perfect in every way but refers to a chain of events which *has already happened*! On one occasion I gave a client a reading in which the events described were quite accurate, but they had happened five years before; but the worst was one which spelled out equally accurately a drama which had occurred *forty years earlier*!

Having said this, the vast majority of readings will show the *current* situation, and then move on to what is to come. A reading will reveal feelings, emotion, changes of direction, important decisions and so on, but if there really is *nothing* going on in the Questioner's life, the reading will reflect this too. Sometimes you simply have to tell a Questioner that the year or so ahead will be quiet and uneventful. However, the following ideas are worth exploring.

Seasons

The Minor Arcana cards can be used as a seasonal guide by dealing out one card from the top of the deck. If this turns out to be a Major card, just keep going until you find the first Minor card and then look to see which suit it is from. Different Readers have different ideas as to which suit might refer to which season and, like everything in Tarot, you will have to follow your own instincts on this. The following idea is purely personal, but it may make enough sense for you to adopt it and use it for yourself.

Spring:
Wands

The Wand cards are illustrated with sprouting branches and so many of them refer to the beginning of new enterprises. This invests them with a 'spring-like' feel.

Summer:
Cups

The ideas of fruition, fullness, warmth and joy which are associated with these cards link well with the lazy days of summer.

Autumn:
Pentacles

These cards have a feeling of wealth, resources and preservation which seem to fit well with the idea of bringing in and storing the harvest.

Winter:
Swords

The qualities of sadness, loss, fear, pain and rejection which are associated with so many of these cards have a wintry feel about them.

Twelve months ahead

Many Tarot Readers use a circular pattern of twelve cards in order to represent the twelve months of the year. This is useful as it can also double as an astrological house spread. The method here is to read each card in turn for each month of the year, paying special attention to those cards which seem to signify major events.

Numbers

Another idea is to use the numbers on the cards as a timing device. You can use the method described above in the seasons section for this, shuffling the deck and dealing out one card on its own. When using this method, the meaning of the card is immaterial, the only thing which counts is the number. Therefore an Ace would be one month from the time of the reading, a Two would be two months etc. Travelling up through the

Court cards, this gives you fourteen months to play with. If you use the Major Arcana for this, you can start with The Fool which would suggest that something is about to happen right away, The Magician one month hence, The Priestess two months hence and so on. This gives you twenty-two months (or twenty-two weeks) to use.

Astrology

Many Tarot Readers are also interested in astrology, but even if you are not, the following ideas could be useful.

Firstly, a variation of the number system as explained above could offer Zodiac signs instead of a number of months as follows:

Ace	♈	Aries
Two	♉	Taurus
Three	♊	Gemini
Four	♋	Cancer
Five	♌	Leo
Six	♍	Virgo
Seven	♎	Libra
Eight	♏	Scorpio
Nine	♐	Sagittarius
Ten	♑	Capricorn
Page	♒	Aquarius
Knight	♓	Pisces

Another Zodiac idea would be to use the Court cards. This has another useful facet in that the Court cards can double up as *people* of a particular sign in addition to suggesting a particular month of the year. The system works as follows:

Fire	King of Wands	Leo
	Queen of Wands	Aries
	Knight of Wands	Sagittarius
Air	King of Swords	Aquarius
	Queen of Swords	Libra
	Knight of Swords	Gemini
Earth	King of Pentacles	Capricorn
	Queen of Pentacles	Taurus
	Knight of Pentacles	Virgo

Water	King of Cups	Scorpio
	Queen of Cups	Cancer
	Knight of Cups	Pisces

Jean Goode's timing device

I demonstrated this method in my previous book *Fortune-Telling by Tarot Cards* but I am happy to repeat it here because I have found it very useful when using the Celtic Cross spread to look at a specific department of a client's life and to time the effects of this event. This method was given to me by a very experienced Reader called Jean Goode who lives and works in Brighton, on the south coast of Britain.

The idea is to lay out the usual Celtic Cross spread (see page 166) using both Arcanas of the Tarot. Then work *backwards* through the spread until you reach a Minor Arcana card which is not a Court card. Then work out your timing like this:

Years are indicated by a Pentacle card.
Months are indicated by a Sword card.
Weeks are indicated by a Wand card.
Days are indicated by a Cup card *but only if it is next to a Pentacle card*!

Jean tells me that she usually encounters her first such numbered card among the four cards which are alongside the Cross itself. If this is not the case, you should just keep working *backwards* until a numbered card is found.

The six-month method

This is a method which I use quite a lot. The cards should be laid out in two rows of six, as per the astrological spread on page 166. If the card representing the event turns up in the six cards on the top row, the event will take place within six months. If it is to be found in the second six cards, on the bottom row, the event will occur between six to twelve months. If there is nothing useful to be found in either row of cards, then deal out another twelve cards and see whether it turns up in the twelve to eighteen month or eighteen to twenty-four month areas. This doesn't pin the Tarot Reader down to an exact time and is, therefore, more likely to be both accurate and useful.

Conclusion

The advice here is to try everything and see what works for you. Be flexible in your approach and use different methods on different occasions. There will be readings when a timespan seems to jump out at you, for example when three cards of the same number present themselves in one short reading.

Chapter 18

Groupings

This chapter harks back a little to the reverse readings in Chapter 9. The idea is to get you thinking about the energies behind *groups* of cards. We have discussed the elements and the four suits but there are cards which seem to relate clearly to a particular aspect of life. Some of these are so obvious that every Tarot Reader would tend to see them the same way. An example of this would be the Death Card, which is universally understood as being a major ending and transformation of some part of one's life. Most of the other cards will change their meaning with each reading and with each person who reads them. The lists below are not something which you should strive to remember, but just another way of stretching your mind and teaching you to associate one card with the others around it. Remember, my interpretations of the cards and my way of grouping them will not necessarily be yours, and yours need not be the same as anyone else's.

I suggest that you create your own list of groups because it is a good way of learning to grasp the meaning of either one card on its own or a combination of similar ones.

Travel

The Knights
Eight of Wands
Six of Swords
The Chariot

Problems with the car

The Chariot
The Knights
Seven of Swords

Holidays

The Sun
Eight of Wands (hot country)
Six of Swords (cold place)
The Empress (the countryside)

Moving on

Eight of Cups
Seven of Swords
Judgement
The World

New house

Two of Wands
Four of Wands
Three of Pentacles
The Empress (especially with land or a garden involved)
The Tower (a problem with property or a loss of one's home)
Five of Pentacles (mortgage difficulties)
Two of Pentacles (mortgage etc.)

Furnishing, decorating, or throwing out wornout objects

Nine of Pentacles

Making a garden

The Empress
Nine of Pentacles

Sex

The Devil
Ace of Swords (power or passion)
Ace of Wands (phallic symbol)

Love and romance

Ace and Two of Cups
The Lovers

Engagement

Two of Cups
Two of Wands

Marriage

Three of Cups
The Hierophant
The Lovers
The Devil (commitment)

Parting

Eight of Cups
Three of Swords
Five of Swords (acrimonious)
Two of Pentacles (especially where money and goods are concerned)

Children

Six of Cups
Ten of Cups
The Pages
The Sun

Parents, worry about them

Nine of Swords
The Moon (the mother, especially)
The Emperor (the father)
The Empress (the mother)

Good friends

Relevant Court cards but Cups are especially favoured

The man in a woman's life

Kings
Knights
The Emperor
The Magician
Any apparently relevant card

The woman in a man's life

Queens
Possibly Knights and Pages
The Empress
The Priestess
The Moon (if all is not going well)

Legal matters

Seven of Swords
Justice
Judgement

Joy, satisfaction

The Sun
Ten of Cups
Nine of Cups
Six of Wands

Loneliness, being happily alone

The Hermit

Disappointment, sadness

Four of Cups
Five of Cups
Ten of Swords
The Moon

Worry, loss

Nine of Swords
Five of Pentacles
Five of Cups
Three of Swords

Muddles, indecision

The Chariot
The Moon
Seven of Cups
Nine of Swords
Two of Swords

Victory

Six of Wands
The Chariot
The Sun
Justice

Judgement
The World

Problems

Seven of Wands
Nine of Wands
Nine of Swords
Eight of Swords
The Hanged Man

Peace, moderation

Temperance

Diplomacy

Strength
Temperance

Sacrifice

The Hanged Man

Things being more or less alright

Nine of Wands
Seven of Wands
Two of Swords
Nine of Cups
Nine of Pentacles

A feeling of imprisonment or being trapped

Nine of Wands
Eight of Swords (can literally
    mean prison)

New job

Three of Pentacles
Eight of Pentacles
Aces
The Devil (commitment)

Money, security

Ace of Pentacles
Four of Pentacles
Ten of Pentacles
Nine of Pentacles
Page of Pentacles

Hard work

Ten of Wands
Seven of Pentacles

Success

The Sun
Six of Wands
Four of Pentacles (exams)

Working partnerships

Two of any suit
Relevant Court cards
The Lovers

A new enterprise, self-employment

Aces
Three of Wands
The Magician
The Star
The Sun (success)

Challenges

Five of Wands
Ace of Swords
Five of Wands
Seven of Wands
The Chariot

Art, creativity, music, hobbies

Page of Cups

Ace of Cups
Ace of Wands
Seven of Wands

Giving, paying debts

Ace of Cups
Six of Pentacles
Two of Pentacles

Swindles, mysteries, lies

The Moon
The Priestess (not really a swindle etc., but being without the full facts)
The Tower (finding out the hard way)
The Hermit (finding out the easy way)
Page of Swords (a word to the wise)

The boss

Relevant Court card
The Emperor

Bank manager or land and property owner

King of Pentacles
Queen of Pentacles
Knight of Pentacles
The Emperor

Ideas

The Magician
The Fool
Ace of Swords

Food

The Empress

Health

Four of Swords
Three of Swords
Strength

Advice given or received

The Hermit
Any appropriate Court card
The Emperor
The Priestess
The Hierophant
Seven of Swords

Doctor, lawyer

King of Swords
Queen of Swords
Knight of Swords

Teacher or advisor

The Hermit
The Hierophant
The Priestess

Letters, news, writing, communicating

Page of Wands
Many of the Wand cards

Education

Page of Cups
Page of Wands
The Priestess
The Star
The Hermit (advisor)
The Hierophant (advisor)

Planning for the future

The Star
The Ace of Swords

New start of any kind

The Fool
The Magician
The Wheel of Fortune
The Star
The World

Endings of any kind

Five of Swords
Ten of Swords
Two of Pentacles
The Wheel of Fortune
Death
The Tower
Judgement
The World

Delay

The Hanged Man
Two of Swords

Spiritual enlightenment

The Priestess
The Magician
The Hierophant
The Hermit
The Devil
The Tower
Ace of Swords

Psychic ability

The Priestess
The Magician
The Hermit
The Hierophant

Psychic inspiration

The Priestess
The Magician

The Hermit
The Hierophant
The Star

The Moon
The Tower
The Devil (reversed)

Chapter 19

An Introduction to Spreads

A good deal of the rest of this book will be dealing with the cards in a variety of specific spreads and layouts. Some spreads are useful for an overall reading, and these I call *comprehensive spreads*. Others are more useful for looking at a specific situation and these I call *focused spreads*, while others are useful for timing events and these I call *calendar spreads*. Some layouts can be used both as comprehensive and calendar spreads, while one or two can double as focused or calendar spreads. Some spreads are more successful than others, therefore in the following chapters, I shall volunteer an opinion and also indicate the best use to which each spreads can be put. At the end of this book you will find 'Sasha's Witch Report' which will give you an instant view of the value of all the spreads which are examined in this book, plus suggestions as to how they can best be used.

The simplest form of spread

The most basic spread is one which allows the Reader to move from the past to the present and then on to the future. Perhaps the easiest way to do this is to take six cards and work forward.

If you want a 'tighter' reading, use two cards for the past, two for the present and two for the future. If you prefer to leave your readings 'loose' just move from one unspecified period of time to another.

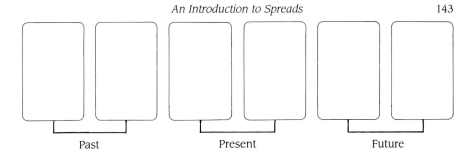

| Past | Present | Future |

This, combined with an observation of the 'loading' of ratios, contents, elements etc. as explained in previous chapters, can make for a nicely accurate little reading. This assessment of the 'loading' or 'weighting' of a reading may seem a longwinded process to you at first, but it will soon become second nature to quickly run your eyes over the layout before opening your mouth to speak.

Answering a question with the Tarot

If you wish to find the answer to a specific question, you will need to choose a particular card to act as the *Significator* of the question. This card may choose itself from some earlier and more comprehensive stage of the reading or you may decide to choose one which represents the situation. For example, if your question was 'Will I get a new job soon?', you would probably choose the Eight of Pentacles as Significator to represent the question. You would then take another two or three cards at random to see what the answer might be.

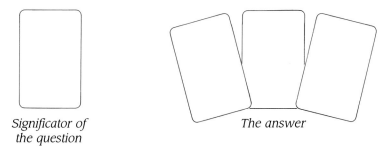

Significator of
the question   The answer

Before moving on, I suggest you try this one out for yourself, either using yourself as guinea-pig or asking a friend to help you. Use the questions in the box as a mind-jogger.

What was your choice of Significator and why?

**What conclusion do you draw from the cards which supply
the answer to the question?**

Spot the problem

Another very simple idea for a trainee Reader is to ask your Questioner
to shuffle the cards and then deal three or four cards from the top of the
deck. See what he or she has picked and try to work out what is worrying
him or her. The following three *Prediction Tarot* cards were picked by my
neighbour who is worried about her husband and children.

PAGE OF SWORDS   PAGE OF COINS   KING OF CUPS

You can try this with seven cards spread out into a random pattern. One card may leap out at you, possibly accompanied by another which is similar. In this case, don't try to interpret all seven of the cards, just concentrate on the one or two to which your attention has been drawn. Now, without saying anything, ask your Questioner to rearrange all the cards so that they form a row. Working from left to right this time, you will be able to see whether the problem has been around for some time or is just coming into being.

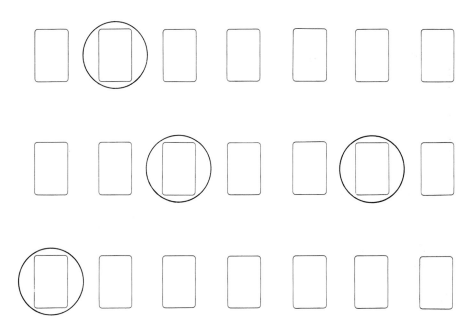

A problem-finding experiment

The above spread is unwieldy and not really recommended for everyday use but it is a good training aid. I have seen it used very successfully by a highly intuitive professional Reader and, on occasion, I have used it myself, but I can think of many easier ways to do the job. The idea is to lay out a large number of cards in a rectangular spread and look over them, allowing the important ones to 'jump out' at you.

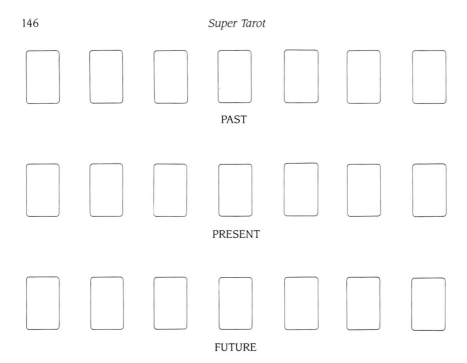

PAST

PRESENT

FUTURE

The Romany Spread

The three-by-seven or 'Romany' spread

Personally, I have never found this spread to be much use but please try it for yourself. The method is to ask your Questioner to shuffle the cards and then to deal out three rows of seven cards. The first row represents the past, the middle one represents the present and the last row represents the future.

Chapter 20

Comprehensive Spreads

If you read my earlier book *Tarot in Action!*, you will see actual readings using some of these spreads, so here I shall simply show you how to use them for yourself.

We have already looked at some spreads in which cards are spread out in a shapeless mass on the table as well as the large 'spot the problem' layout and the Romany three-by-seven layout; now let us look at a couple of others.

The pyramid spread

The pyramid spread is read from the bottom of the pyramid upwards. The base of the pyramid shows the basis of the situation or the past occurrences from which current and future events are bound to develop.

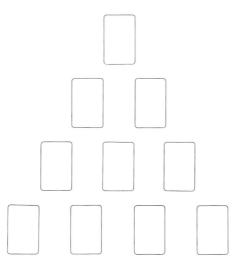

Seven-card spread

The idea here is to place seven cards in a row and read them in a way which suits you. Here are my suggestions for the designation of each card.

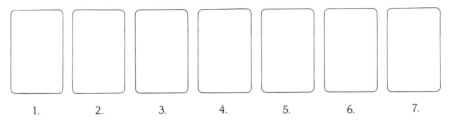

1.   2.   3.   4.   5.   6.   7.

1st card	The state of the Questioner's mind.
2nd card	What others are doing to him or want from him.
3rd card	Events close to home.
4th card	Events in the Questioner's world outside the home.
5th card	The past.
6th card	The future.
7th card	The outcome.

Personal-choice spread

This is a good layout for a beginner to experiment with. I have demonstrated this idea in both my previous books and still think that after you have practised with the four-card readings, as described in earlier chapters, this is the best one to play with. The idea is to use a smallish number of cards and to designate the positions in which you place them so that each relates to a situation. It would be a good idea to make up some simple design on a piece of paper and write the designations on it. The design could be a single row of six cards, two rows of four or a circular layout or, indeed, anything else which appeals to you. When you have sorted out your preferred layout, ask one of your friends to act as Questioner and get her to shuffle the cards and pick out whatever number you have chosen for your spread. She should then hand the cards to you so that you can lay them out on the pattern.

I have provided you with some notes to study just in case you need a 'bump start'. If you feel that you can cope with this reading on your own, don't bother to read my note section.

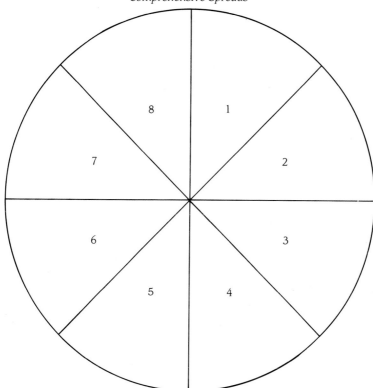

The designations which I have suggested are as follows:

1. Money
2. Career
3. Home
4. Children
5. Health
6. Travel
7. Hobbies
8. Change or stasis

The cards chosen by my Questioner were as follows:

1. The Empress
2. The Hermit
3. Queen of Pentacles
4. Seven of Wands
5. Nine of Pentacles
6. Ten of Cups
7. Four of Cups
8. Page of Cups

Notes and brief interpretation of Robert's cards

The cards, taken from Anthony Clark's *Magickal Tarot*, are generally good. There are two Major cards in an eight-card layout which shows that, although fate is taking a hand with his life, he is still able to dictate how things go for himself. The high ratio of Cup cards show that he is approaching life from an emotional point of view and could therefore be subject to fits of anger and depression or joy and euphoria depending upon events. He will have to apply far more logic and less emotion to his circumstances. The Pentacle cards bode well for his future finances, especially in the home area. The Seven of Wands and Four of Cups show that problems will have to be faced but they are not overwhelming.

1. The Empress in connection with money is a good omen as it suggests fruitfulness and abundance etc.

2. The Hermit in connection with the career suggests that Robert will have time to reflect upon where he is going and what he wants to do in future. He will receive advice and will gain enlightenment.

3. The Queen of Pentacles in the home area suggests a capable wife who has her own source of wealth.

4. The Seven of Wands in the area of children shows that he will have some problems here but that they are not insurmountable.

5. The Nine of Pentacles in the area of health shows nothing to worry about, but nevertheless he should get out of doors and into the garden when he can.

6. The Ten of Cups in the area of travel shows great happiness in this aspect of life.

7. The Four of Cups in the area of hobbies shows
    that he is not terribly satisfied by them or lacks
    interest in them.

8. The Page of Cups in the area of change or stasis
    suggests that new things will shortly need to be
    learned, and consequently that changes are on
    the way.

The element spread

This spread was suggested to me by my friend, Seldiy Bate, who has a very
great interest in spiritual matters. Ask your Questioner to shuffle the cards
and deal out five piles containing three cards. The first pile is associated
with *earth*, the second with *air*, the third with *fire*, the fourth with *water* and
the fifth with *spirit*. (If you need to revise the ideas behind the elements,
look back to Chapter 4.)

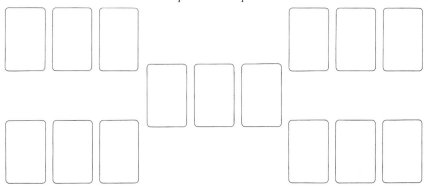

Because this is such an interesting idea, I think we should take the time to work through a reading together. I asked my son, Stuart, to pick the cards for this reading because at that time he was at an interesting point in his life. He picked from *The Arthurian Tarot*.

The cards which Stuart found himself with were as follows:

Earth	Ace of Cups	*Water*	Eight of Wands
	The Sun		Knight of Wands
	Ace of Swords		Seven of Swords
Air	Knight of Swords	*Spirit*	Eight of Pentacles
	Five of Wands		The Chariot
	Ten of Wands		King of Wands
Fire	The Star		
	Nine of Wands		
	The Emperor		

Each group of cards has to be interpreted separately and in relation to the element to which it has been assigned. It is also worth following our natural inclination to look at each group from left to right. Therefore, the earth group would signify new beginnings which will have a very happy outcome and which will improve the practical and financial side of his life. The air group suggests movement, challenge and a lot of hard work and is connected to the world of ideas, serious decisions and worries. The reading suggests that he will have to use his mind energetically but would find the challenge rewarding. However, a good deal of responsibility and worry will be inevitable.

The fire group suggests great hope for the future and many plans to be made; troubles will come but, because he is operating from a firm base, these should not be overwhelming. He will become a stronger and more powerful person as a result of all the running around and communicating which he will soon have to cope with. The water group suggests that travel will become important to his emotional life and that people from afar will influence his feelings. Communications, the use of language, and sales or instruction work will be important to him. He will soon be moving on, which will make him feel a little sad and homesick but will enable him to build his own life for the future. The spirit trilogy tells us that he will have to work hard on earth for a long time before thinking of joining the spirit world but that he does have an understanding of, and a strong link with, the 'other side'. It is clear that my father, whom Stuart resembles, is looking after his progress. He understands the laws of karma and the workings of the spiritual world and, although intensely materialistic and practical in outlook, he will always have that secret psychic or spiritual connection to fall back on.

Now I will satisfy your curiosity by telling you how well this matches Stuart's current and future situation at the time of the reading. He was twenty-one years old and nearing the end of a degree course in computer and business studies. He had kept himself in pocket money over the previous couple of years by running a small computer business, and he had enjoyed that very much. He had gone on holiday with a pal the year before, during which time the two lads met two Swiss sisters. This meeting lead to a deepening relationship between the two sisters and the two young men.

Chapter 21

More Comprehensive Spreads

By now you will have realized that a comprehensive spread is one which takes a look at the Questioner's position as a whole without focusing upon any particular aspect of it. These spreads can be very simple as described in Chapter 19 or extremely complicated, as we shall see shortly. The interpretation of some spreads relies upon the Reader having other forms of esoteric knowledge, such as astrology, numerology or the Kabbala. I shall describe some of these briefly here but if you want to see them working in more detail, I suggest that you have a look at my own earlier books or those written by Rachel Pollack.

The Horseshoe spread

I expect you have seen this spread used in films and television plays. It involves laying a horseshoe-shaped double line of cards on the table. I have never seen this layout used professionally, and personally consider it to be far too cumbersome for serious use. I wonder if you can remember the James Bond film in which this spread was used (I believe it was *Live and Let Die*). In the story, Solitaire, the Tarot Reader, picked out the Lovers card from the side of the horseshoe and foretold the fatal romance between herself and Bond. He, of course, had a pack which was made up entirely of Lovers cards. (Incidentally, the pack which was used for that part of the film was the Witches' Tarot whilst the cards which were used at the beginning of the film were of the Rider Waite variety.)

The layout used at the very beginning of the film was a carbon copy of Seldiy Bate's element spread but used in a different way. As Solitaire laid out the cards she said: 'A man comes' (this was the Knight of Wands); 'He comes over water' (the Six of Swords); 'He comes with a purpose' (the Knight of Swords); 'He brings chaos and destruction' (The Tower).

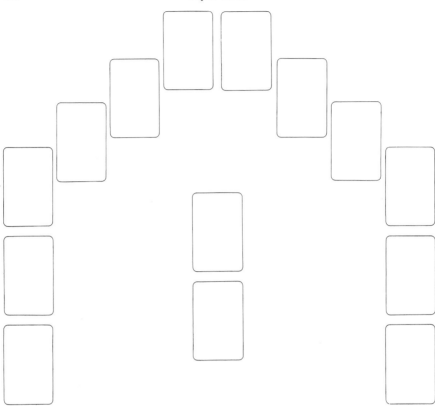

The Tree of Life spread

This spread requires a thorough understanding of the Kabbala, so if you are interested, I suggest that you get together with people who understand Kabbalistic techniques and see whether you can work with them. The details of the system given below have been provided for me by Douglas Ashby, who is a teacher of the Kabbala.

The Tree of Life is made up of ten Sephiroth plus one extra. Each of the Sephiroth has a series of meanings within it and is also like a computer sub-directory, which means that it carries within it an extended Tree system which can be used for further and deeper study of the system. It originated in central Europe amongst religious Jews who were looking for a system of understanding the workings of the universe and an esoterically spiritual way of life.

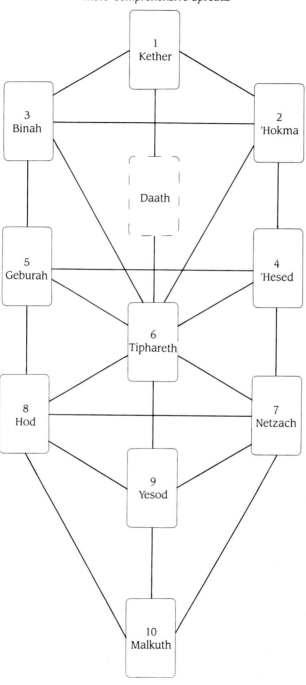

Description of the Tree of Life

The names shown on the diagram are the traditional Hebrew ones, and the descriptions given below are only a few of the many different attributes allocated to each of the Sephiroth. These will suffice for our present purposes, though.

Kether	Spiritual impulse, higher self, spiritual influences surrounding one, the roots of new things due to come into one's life. Conception of anything. The four Aces.
'Hokma	Male image, how one relates to the active male force, new things beginning to come into being. Left side of the head. First month of pregnancy. Father. The four Twos.
Binah	Feminine image, how one relates to the receptive, structuring processes of life, right side of the head, second month of pregnancy. Mother. The four Threes.
'Hesed	Ideals, the law, religious matters, one's inner will, planning processes, compassionate nature, left shoulder and arm, third month of pregnancy. Female relatives. The four Fours.
Geburah	Active aspirations, ability to act, determination, strength, ability to destroy the past in order to create the future, right shoulder and arm, fourth month of pregnancy. Male relatives. The four Fives.
Tiphareth	Control, balance, harmony, heart centre, centre of being, lungs, solar plexus, active will, things now definitely in the process of coming to fruition. The fifth month of pregnancy. Husband in female reading. The four Sixes.
Netzach	Emotional nature, feelings, desires, artistic creativity, romance, left hand and hip-back-loin, sons, the sixth month of pregnancy. The four Sevens.

Hod	Thoughts, communication, speech, logic, right hand and hip-back-loins, sons, the seventh month of pregnancy. The four Eights.
Yesod	Imagination, instincts, habit patterns, sex, food, home environment, sexual organs. Eighth month of pregnancy. Wife in a male reading. The four Nines.
Malkuth	General physical condition and environment, what is happening now and just past, legs and feet. All things which have now come into manifestation or which are passing away. The ninth month of pregnancy. Birth and death. The four Tens.

Numerological spreads

A numerological approach can be used in various spreads the first of which is similar to the astrological spread because it gives an overview of the Questioner's situation. The basic idea is to use nine cards and look at them in the context of their numerological positions. Many numerologists also use the numbers eleven and twenty-two, which are considered especially significant, but for the purposes of this reading, nine cards are sufficient.

1. Ambition, action, aggressive energy, mental 'muscle', the start of an enterprise.
2. Partnership, harmony, peace and moderation. The start of a new relationship.
3. Creativity, new beginnings which involve other people, material benefits to come from partnerships. Possibly the birth of a child.
4. Security, practicalities, the foundation of anything, also restrictions and limitations, parents, authority figures, a workable routine.
5. Activity, the need to break out of an established routine, travel, change, marketing oneself or one's products.
6. Home and family, duties and ties, giving love, warmth, food and security. Harmony, health and caring for the welfare of others.
7. Rest, relaxation and time off to think things over. The occult or religious and spiritual ideas. Reflection and analysis.
8. Material success and also spiritual attainment. Progress and balance

between the two, bringing achievement and success. Money and business matters will prosper.

9. Perfection, completion, detached love, humanitarianism. The end of a phase, the loss of some aspect of one's life which clears the way for another cycle to begin. Reaching a higher level in one's spiritual attainment, improving one's karma.

The following is a brief example using *The Celtic Tarot.*

1. *Judgement* This card would suggest that rather than starting an enterprise, a longstanding course of action is being brought to an end. The reversed stance of this card suggests that it is the action of others rather than of the Reader which is responsible for this situation.
2. *Page of Wands* A partnership in connection with writing, communicating and education is about to start.
3. *Ace of Pentacles* A new beginning which involves others and which will be financially beneficial.
4. *Ten of Pentacles* The financial and working aspects of the future look secure.
5. *Nine of Cups* A change of direction will be satisfactory and pleasurable.
6. *The Moon* There will be unexpected problems and benefits in the area of the home and family. Something is not quite right here but the

situation is not ready to reveal itself yet. Something to do with water may cause a problem.

7. *Eight of Pentacles* The spiritual side of life will bring some kind of new or more important work into being. There will be little time for rest or relaxation.

8. *Eight of Wands reversed* The reversed aspect of this card shows that although the Questioner will be extremely successful, the workload may be too heavy and may not lead to any kind of personal growth.

9. *Page of Cups* Something completely new will come of these changes which will bring some kind of emotional or spiritual satisfaction. There will be new methods to be learned and new people entering and influencing the Questioner's life.

The three-card oraculum

You can use numerology and the Tarot as a simple oraculum by taking three cards, adding their numbers together and seeing what you have. If your total is twenty-two or less, then refer to the Major Arcana card which corresponds to the number which you have. If the number exceeds twenty-two, reduce the total as demonstrated below to see which Major Arcana card it refers to. The following example will show you what I mean; it is illustrated with three of the striking — if rather unorthodox — cards from *The Merlin Tarot* which correspond with the cards mentioned:

SERPENTS

Misfortune

Benefit

Queen of Wands	13
Nine of Swords	9
Six of Pentacles	6
	28

2 + 8 = 10 The tenth Major card would be The Wheel of Fortune, so the

advice to the Questioner would be to expect changes and to make use of them in a positive manner.

The I Ching

It is possible to do the same sort of thing with the *I Ching*. You will need an *I Ching Book of Changes* for this or, alternatively, a copy of my *Fortune-Teller's Workbook* which includes an abbreviated and anglicized version of it.

This is a totally original idea which can be experimented with. There are sixty-four numbers in the I Ching hexagrams, so let us see which number a group of three cards would give us:

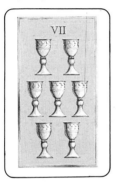  

Seven of Cups	7
The Hierophant	5
Judgement	20
	32

The thirty-second hexagram of the I Ching reads something like this: 'Stay put, persevere and allow things to take their course. Hastiness will bring problems. Don't insist on having things all your own way, a casual attitude would be far better. Wait, be yourself and you will get all that you want.'

The astrological spread

This spread is used by a great many Tarot Readers, even those who have very little true astrological knowledge. It is my personal favourite and I always begin my readings with it in order to gain an overview of the Questioner's current and future circumstances. The layout and astrological 'house' position meanings are as follows:

The Questioner The body and appearance People closely affecting the Questioner if a Court card falls here 1	Money and possessions Values 2	Local affairs Siblings and neighbours Education Communications 3	Home Mother Premises both home and work 4	Children Amusements Lovers Enterprises Speculation in either business or other gambles 5	Work/service Health Hospitals Bosses and employees 6
Partners Relationships Marriage 7	Corporate or shared money Deep side of life Birth and death Sex, relationships where sex is very important 8	Travel and foreigners The law Religion/Mysticism Higher education Outdoor life/horses 9	Status Career Aims Father 10	Friends Clubs Intellectual Hobbies 11	Inner self Psyche Inner peace/terror 12

The Jung spread

I have demonstrated this in a previous book but I will explain its use here for the benefit of those of you who are interested in transactional analysis. The idea is to take one card to represent the Questioner (see the notes on uses of a significator in Chapter 13). Then take two cards each for the animus, anima and the child. The animus is the father figure within all of us who tells us what we should be doing whether we want to or not. The anima is the mother figure in all of us who reminds us of our duty to ourselves and to humanity; while the child is the hidden side which reveals what we *really* want.

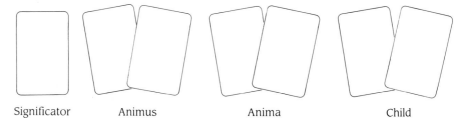

Significator   Animus   Anima   Child

Annual or timing spreads

In this case, start at the twelve o'clock position and take one card for each month of the year ahead.

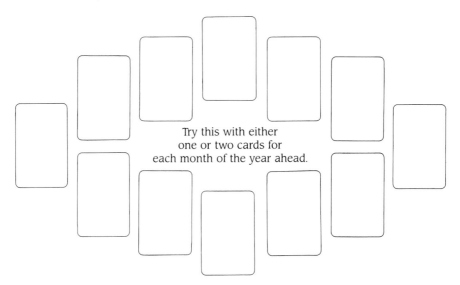

Try this with either
one or two cards for
each month of the year ahead.

Spreads Which Focus on a Particular Problem or Situation

The pathways spread

This will show Questioners what would happen if they chose one of two paths forward. The example below is given in answer to the question, 'Shall I change my job or stay where I am?'

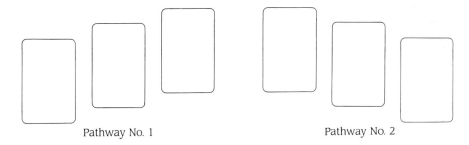

Pathway No. 1   Pathway No. 2

The consequences spread

This is another very useful spread which I use constantly. It was first demonstrated to me by a Reader called Christina Artemis.

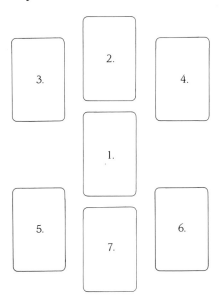

The spread works like this.

1. The person or situation.
2. What is for or against him.
3. The past.
4. The future.
5. Suggested direction to go in.
6. The surrounding environment or the actions of others.
7. The outcome.

There are examples of this spread in both of my previous books on the Tarot. This spread can be used with the Major Arcana cards on their own or with the whole pack.

The Celtic Cross spread

This ever-popular spread can be used with the whole pack or with the

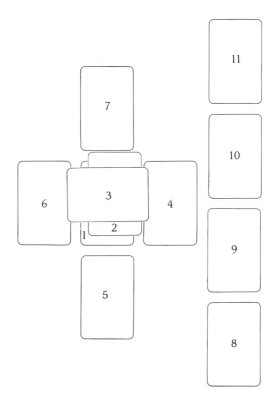

Major Arcana cards only. I have gone into it in detail in both my previous books and I think it must appear in almost every book written on the Tarot. Just for the record, I shall go over the layout once again. If you find that the order in which I read the cards is a little different from that in some other books don't worry, there is quite a considerable variation in the way that this spread is read by different Readers.

The spread works as follows:

1. The Significator (see Chapter 13).
2. The Questioner's present situation.
3. Whatever is causing or influencing the situation.
4. People or events which will figure in the life of the Questioner in the near future.
5. The distant past.
6. The recent past.
7. The goal, aim or ideal. Alternatively, the best that the Questioner can hope for under the present circumstances.
8. More information about the Questioner and how he or she affects the surrounding environment.
9. Other people or situations around the Questioner and how *they* affect the Questioner.
10. Inner feelings, hopes and fears.
11. Outcome.

Conclusion

I seriously considered ending this book with a spoof exam paper, but I decided that if you have managed to cope with the exercises in this book, you will have reached the standard required to pass any kind of exam — if there were such a thing for the Tarot. If you are still having problems just keep going, because Tarot is a skill which requires practice. When I was teaching myself how to use the cards, I added a Tarot reading on to the end of all my clients' palmistry or astrology readings. I explained to each client what I was doing and that the service was free of charge. They all happily co-operated, and after about three months I felt that I had become sufficiently comfortable with the cards to begin making a small charge for reading them. Nowadays, I give more Tarot readings than anything else because I find them so good at pinpointing problems, areas of potential growth, potential joy and happiness and every other human condition. If a reading doesn't work out immediately, leave the cards where they are on the table, ask your Questioner a question or two in order to clarify matters, and backtrack over the cards to see if you can pick up the story from there.

I hope that this book has gone some way to answer the many queries I have had from people asking how to improve their ability to string the cards together to make a story. I also hope that the exercises and the experiments on your friends, neighbours and colleagues help you to gain confidence and develop your imagination and your powers of creativity. Above all, you must choose the methods which work for *you* and use your own experience of life. If you need more help in this direction, invest in a good counselling course. Remember that Tarot Readers cannot distance themselves in the same way as a counsellor but must become involved in their clients' pain and pleasures. Finally, please remember that this book is only a guideline and not an unchanging tablet of stone.

Appendix

The Witch Report on Tarot Spreads

SPREADS	Compre-hensive	Focused	Easy to use	Needs other skills	Requires a Significator	Notes should be made	Clear answers obtained	One which I use myself
Random	✓		✓			✓		✓
Radio	✓		✓				✓	✓
Simple	✓		✓				✓	✓
Q & A		✓	✓		✓		✓	✓
Spot the problem	✓					✓	✓	✓
Spot the events	✓					✓		✓
Gypsy	✓					✓		
Pyramid	✓					✓	✓	
Seven-card	✓		✓			✓	✓	
Personal	✓		✓			✓		
Element	✓			✓		✓	✓	
Horseshoe	✓					✓		
Tree of Life	✓			✓		✓		
Astrology	✓			✓		✓	✓	✓
Numerology	✓			✓		✓	✓	
Oraculum	✓			✓			✓	
I Ching		✓	✓	✓			✓	
Jung		✓			✓	✓	✓	
Annual			✓				✓	✓
Pathways		✓	✓			✓	✓	✓
Consequences		✓	✓		✓	✓	✓	✓
Celtic Cross		✓			✓	✓	✓	✓

Further Reading

The Prediction Tarot Pack

Sasha Fenton (*The Aquarian Press, 1990*)

This pack contains my best-selling *Fortune-Telling by Tarot Cards* book (also available on its own) and the hugely popular *Prediction Tarot* deck, conceived by Bernard Stringer and painted by Peter Richardson. As individual items each has sold over 100,000 copies — now together they make a unique introduction to the Tarot.

Tarot in Action!

Sasha Fenton (*The Aquarian Press, 1987*)

This book is aimed at all those people who want to improve their fluency in using Tarot spreads. Providing detailed descriptions of a selection of spreads, from the simple to the complex, and giving word-for-word accounts of real-life readings by way of example, *Tarot in Action!* will give encouragement to novices and inspiration to experts.

Discover Tarot

Emily Peach (*The Aquarian Press, 1990*)

This book is a radical new approach to understanding and using the Tarot. First published in 1984 as *The Tarot Workbook*, it contains a carefully graded course of practical exercises designed to give the student a sound working knowledge of Tarot symbolism and interpretation in the shortest possible time.

The Norse Tarot Pack

Clive Barrett (*The Aquarian Press, 1989*)

Breaking new ground in Tarot conception, this original deck — beautifully painted by author Clive Barrett — uses Viking mythology to convey traditional Tarot meanings. The accompanying book stresses the importance of the gods, sagas and runes in the early Norse way of life and offers a new angle on interpreting and reading the Tarot.

Tarot for Relationships

Jocelyn Almond & Keith Seddon (*The Aquarian Press, 1990*)

The Tarot is the key to finding out about yourself and your emotional needs, and in this book particular emphasis is placed upon its use to provide guidance in close personal relationships. For both beginners and experienced card readers, the book gives both traditional and sexual interpretations and is illustrated with the *Norse Tarot.*

The Merlin Tarot Pack

R.J. Stewart (*The Aquarian Press, 1988*)

This unique Tarot concept is based on the adventures of Merlin, drawn directly from authentic twelfth-century sources. These cards, superbly illustrated by Miranda Gray, are unequalled tools for visualization, meditation and prediction, and come packaged with R.J. Stewart's book of images, insight and wisdom from the age of Merlin.

The New Tarot

Rachel Pollack (*The Aquarian Press, 1989*)

This lavish book catalogues over 70 Tarot decks produced in the last 20 years to demonstrate how the Tarot has evolved. Rachel Pollack critically evaluates the themes and styles used by today's designers, indicating their strengths and weaknesses and comparing them with the traditional decks which have inspired them.

The Arthurian Tarot Pack

John & Caitlín Matthews
(*The Aquarian Press, 1990*)

Steeped in the magic, legends and history of Arthurian Britain, these exceptional cards capture all the wonder and beauty of King Arthur's realm. Beautifully executed by Miranda Gray, this original pack comes complete with a fully-illustrated guide to meanings and spreads; a more advanced handbook for the cards, *Hallowquest*, is also available.

Tarot: A New Handbook for the Apprentice

Eileen Connolly (*The Aquarian Press, 1986*)

This book has established itself as a modern classic on the interpretation of the Tarot in relation to the Qabalah, astrology and numerology. Whatever your purpose in studying the Tarot, this handbook will provide a continual point of reference and will enable students to work with and understand the Tarot.

Tarot: The Handbook for the Journeyman

Eileen Connolly (*The Aquarian Press, 1990*)

In this second volume of Eileen Connolly's best-selling Tarot series, the student advances on the upward path from Apprentice to Journeyman. Her new *Conjunction* concept provides deeper insights for establishing the timing of events, and the book shows how to incorporate the focusing power of crystals in your readings.

The Celtic Tarot Pack

Courtney Davis & Helena Paterson
(*The Aquarian Press, 1990*)

An inspired and superlative blending of Celtic art and Tarot wisdom, this pack combines the unsurpassed elegance of Courtney Davis's world-famous designs with the ancient symbol and magic of Celtic lore. Complete with a book of meanings and spreads, the result is a pack which will delight and enthral lovers of Tarot, mythology and Celtic art.

The Servants of the Light Tarot Pack

Dolores Ashcroft-Nowicki (*The Aquarian Press, 1991*)

The Servants of the Light is renowned as one of the leading schools of magical science. Skilfully realized by artists Jo Gill and Anthony Clark, this book/deck pack is a tool for divination and meditation which is destined to become one of the most influential of all Tarots. A companion book of Tarot meditations, *Inner Landscapes*, is also available.

Seventy-Eight Degrees of Wisdom, Volumes 1 & 2

Rachel Pollack (*The Aquarian Press, 1980, 1983*)

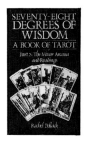

This two-volume work is a widely-praised analysis of the Tarot as a world of potent symbols — a path to self-knowledge, personal growth and freedom. Dealing in turn with the Major and Minor Arcanas, the books demystify Tarot interpretation and make its symbolism an effective and accessible means of self-enlightenment.

Tarot Readings and Meditations

Rachel Pollack (*The Aquarian Press, 1990*)

Following on from her *Seventy-Eight Degrees of Wisdom*, Rachel Pollack presents interpretations and commentaries of a collection of readings undertaken during recent years. The approach is exhaustive, yet specific, going steadily deeper into the cards and the patterns they form, and shows how to go *beyond* the readings.

The Magickal Tarot

Anthony Clark (*The Aquarian Press, 1986*)

This stunning Tarot deck uses a radical interpretation of the symbolism from Aleister Crowley's *Book of Thoth*. Containing an instruction booklet complete with spreads for use with the deck, it offers a unique alternative to more traditional Tarot decks. A separate book by Tony Willis, *Magick and the Tarot*, is also available.